Praise for *Confessions of a Chris[*

"If you are a Christian leader w
Asperger's, autism, or parenting a child with special needs—read this
book! Stephanie Holmes has been a great contributor to the 50,000-
member American Association of Christian Counselors as a speaker
and as part of our Childhood 2.0 course. Now, her counseling and
clinical experience is tied together with her personal journey as a
parent of a special needs child. There is much to learn through
Stephanie's story and spiritual perspectives. I believe this book will
help clinicians, parents, pastors, and other church leaders better
understand, love, and serve individuals and families impacted by
autism spectrum disorders. This book is a gift to helping
professionals and families."

*Tim Clinton, Ed. D. (The College of William and Mary) is president
of the nearly 50,000-member American Association of Christian
Counselors (AACC), the largest and most diverse Christian
counseling association in the world. He is Professor of Counseling
and Pastoral Care and Executive Director of the Center for
Counseling and Family Studies at Liberty University. Licensed in
Virginia as both a Professional Counselor (LPC) and Marriage and
Family Therapist (LMFT).*

"Throughout twenty years of pastoral ministry, I have journeyed with
a number of couples in the challenges of infertility as well as
developmental issues with their children. Each issue can be an
overwhelming burden to the faint of heart. However, I have rarely
dealt with families who have encountered both challenges, yet I am
privileged to have witnessed the grace of God in the life of the
Holmes family as they overcame each of these issues with strength
and dignity. Please understand that overcoming does not necessarily
mean a "fairytale" ending. Instead, overcoming allows someone to
arrive at a place where they can say with the old hymn of the church,
"It is well with my soul." I am confident that as you read this book,
the same God who held the Holmes family within His grip of grace
will be felt in your heart as well. Take hope and courage from the
account of a real family as you see yourself in their struggle to make

sense of the difficulties of life."

Pastor Mark Merrill
Lead Pastor of The Assembly, Warner Robin, Georgia

"Every Christian's relationship with God begins with the conclusion that "God is." As we journey through life, there are times when we must hold to the simple truth that He is without the certainty of where He is or what He is doing. Stephanie Holmes transparently shares her story, which is much more common than might be realized on the surface. Even while her experience is common, it is made all the more valuable because it is God's story being portrayed in her life. Readers will be captured by this author's raw honesty and her ability to talk about the struggles of parenting an autistic child without denying that "God is," and, if we seek Him, He may be found."

Richard D. Collins,
Superintendent of the Georgia Assemblies of God

"I am honored Stephanie asked me to review the research and clinical aspect of the appendices. I found her research to be valid, reliable, compelling, and intriguing. I found myself reading the entire book and literally laughed, cried, raged, and rejoiced for Stephanie and her family. This is a must read for every Christian family who has a special needs child, especially with autism spectrum disorder. I give my highest recommendation both clinically and spiritually."

F.G. Hutchings III, Ed.D, LPC, LMFT
Licensed Psychologist

Confessions of a

Christian Counselor

How infertility and autism grew my faith

Stephanie C. Holmes, MA, BCCC,

Certified Autism Specialist

Highway 51 Publishing, LLC
Mint Hill, North Carolina
HWY51.com

Published by Highway 51 Publishing, LLC
Mint Hill, North Carolina
HWY51.com

ISBN: 0-9960570-4-8
ISBN-13: 978-0-9960570-4-2

Library of Congress Control Number: 2015947759

Although the stories told in this book are true, some names have been changed or omitted to protect the privacy of individuals.

Front and back cover design: Steven Mast, Glyph Design Group, glyphdesigngroup.com
Editing: Jerri Menges

Contents

Acknowledgments

First of all, I thank my Lord and Savior for never giving up on me. Thank You for giving me grace, hope, strength, and wisdom.

To my husband, Dan: Thank you for your love and patience. Thank you for pushing me to finish this book, even when I was snarky about it.

To my favorite Aspie, Sydney: You have taught me so much. I am thankful to have you as my daughter. You not only have taught me how to better help others on the spectrum, your life and words serve as a role model to others both on the spectrum and "neurotypical."

To my youngest, Erica: Thank you for being joy and fun and the breath of fresh of air I needed in difficult times. Thank you for being loving, kind, and accepting of people who are different.

To Pawpaw, Mawmaw, Grammy, and Honey: For unconditional grandparent love, your prayers, your time, your support, and your willingness to learn new things about ASD.

To Aunt Rusty and Uncle David for providing a place for Dan to stay during our transition.

To our former Life.Net group, whom we consider our extended family: Thank you for your prayers and support, but most important, your acceptance. Thank you for intercessory prayers on our behalf.

To my Calvary Church staff and family: Thank you for allowing us rest, healing, and a safe place during our time of hurting.

To my friends: You know who you are. You came to my house, called, or emailed me when I was low, and you would not respond to my barricades or fortresses when I tried to isolate myself. You rejoiced with me in victories and cried with me when I felt defeated.

For our advocates: Autism Society of North Carolina and TEACCH.

For therapists, doctors, counselors, and pastors who were part of our journey.

To the wonderful staff, teacher teams, and administrators we had at Peachtree Charter Middle School and Dunwoody High School who believed in my daughter and had a great impact on our lives for the better.

To game changers at crucial points in our journey: Teresa Hucko, Dawn Patterson, Mark and Gretchen Merrill, "Ms. M" Gina Monteleone, Terry Shores, Heather Hackett, and Janet Vickers.

To the American Association of Christian Counselors (AACC): Thank you for giving me a platform to educate clinicians, pastors, and people-helpers about ASD Marriage and Family Issues.

To those who have been a true friend to my daughter, showed kindness, defended her, or stood by her in difficult times: I am forever grateful!

Introduction

For the last four years, God has opened many doors for me to share my story. However, as many preachers have said, "You have seen the glory, but you don't know my story." It would be easy for someone to hear my one-hour presentation and feel as if somehow I had a secret hotline to God, had all the answers, and was well prepared for the journey I was about to take with my daughter. A journey, mind you, that I did not sign up to take, a journey completely off the well-mapped path of life I had already chosen. This is frightening to a control freak such as me. At many points in the journey, I was being refined. I could not see the preparation until I had the 20/20 view of hindsight. The mile markers of the journey tell how autism affected my faith. In fact, my journey did not even begin in the counseling field or field of special needs at all.

Since before I can remember, my career plan was to become a lawyer. I wanted to prosecute domestic violence and child abuse cases; I wanted justice for women and children who had to live under any kind of abuse. This desire grew out of my watching someone very close to me struggle with an alcoholic father. She eventually got away from him, only to end up dating someone who was an addict. This man was emotionally cruel, exploitive, and physically abusive to my friend. I wanted to rescue her. I wanted desperately for her to be free of him, but I was just a teenager.

In my quest to become a lawyer, I took some psychology classes in college to better understand the human mind. I wanted to know why people do what they do, why they choose certain relationships. I began reading books and attending seminars on abusive relationships.

In the summer of 1993, I took a social psychology course back home at the University of North Carolina at Charlotte, and that's when I encountered the story of Kitty Genovese. Twenty-eight-year-old Kitty Genovese was returning home from a night shift in New York City at 3:20 a.m. when she was grabbed by a man, raped, and eventually murdered as thirty-eight neighbors watched from their apartment windows. The first call to the police was not made until 3:50 a.m.—thirty minutes after the initial attack—when Kitty stopped calling out for help and it was suspected she was dead. The investigation showed that the perpetrator had returned at least twice and, seeing no one coming to Kitty's rescue, he continued to brutalize her.

When the eyewitnesses were questioned, they were asked why they didn't call the police. Did they fear retaliation? No. They each could see another neighbor watching, and they each assumed the other neighbor would call for help. No one assumed responsibility for this young woman's life.

When I read that story, I thought for sure it must have been embellished to stretch the point, as part of our psychology class covered diffusion of responsibility. Surely, thirty-eight people did not allow a woman to die! This was before the Internet, so I decided to go to the main library in downtown Charlotte, where microfilm and microfiche were stored. I searched for hours and was about to give up when there it was in the New York Times, an article written by Martin Gansberg on March 27, 1964. Gansberg painted a far more gruesome picture of what had truly happened to Kitty. As I read the details of how the neighbors knew exactly what times the man had returned and the details they observed, I was convinced this woman died because thirty-eight people thought someone else would intervene and save her life.

My sense of justice demands such crimes and debauchery be punished. But the Lord began to speak to me through the Holy Spirit. He said, "Vengeance is mine … I will repay" (Romans 12:19). But it was Romans 12:20 that pierced my heart. "On the contrary, if your enemy is hungry, feed him. If he is thirsty, give him something to drink." And then verse 21: "Do not be overcome by evil, but overcome evil with good."

As I teared up in the library that day, I prayed, "God, this is what

I want to do! I want to overcome evil with good by prosecuting perpetrators and helping the victim."

But God began to teach me that putting away the perpetrator is only a temporary fix for the victim. The victims need help overcoming the abuse and the wounds it incurs. Who would share God's love with them? Who would tell them that no matter what had happened to them, God loved them and He alone could restore them and heal them?

What was God trying to tell me? Did He want me to change my major from pre-law to psychology, this late in the game? By this time, I was engaged, with a wedding date planned for after my graduation date. This brought the concept of cognitive dissonance into full play for me. I believed one thing but was behaving in a way that was completely opposite. I had to decide if I was going to live my life God's way or my way. Would I help victims and fulfill my calling my way through the law or His way, through counseling?

I am pretty strong-willed, so I decided to double major, in psychology and pre-law so I could keep plan B open. I was very conflicted. When I would tell someone I was double majoring and still might go to law school, I would start crying. It was not until I dropped the pre-law major and changed my schedule to all psychology classes that I had peace of mind.

God was changing my well-laid-out plans, which is hard for a Type A personality control freak. But He wanted me in counseling. His job would be vengeance and justice; mine would be to speak healing words through the guidance of the Holy Spirit. This is how victims would get everlasting peace. I set my life plan and career goals to chart that new course. Little did I know the reason God changed my life's path. Little did I know that the training I would receive in counseling would be useful for future events in my personal life and family.

As you read this book, my heart's desire is that no matter how similar or different your situation with a special needs child, you will see my humanness and God's sovereignty in all things; but even more than that—hope! My challenge was to write a book that shared my struggles, my journey, my challenges, my poor choices, and my reliance on God, as honestly and transparently as possible. Parent to parent, or family member to family member, our stories probably have many differences, but our feelings and journey may look the same.

As Scripture says, "Therefore there is now no condemnation for those who are in Christ Jesus" (Romans 8:1). I pray you do not see judgment in this book. I wish to validate your feelings and acknowledge that I had my own struggles. As a counselor, I want to convey that there is *hope*. I want to convey that no matter where you are in your journey, it is okay to seek help, support, and resources, and to have good days and bad days.

As an ordained minister, I truly believe *hope* and help come from above, through a relationship with our Heavenly Father who has a plan for you and your special needs loved one, and who reminds us all that we are made in His image, created equally. Clinically, I hope the resources in the appendices at the end of the book will shed light on various issues that arise when you have a spectrum child across the lifespan.

In this book, you will see that my struggles started way before Asperger's entered our lives. I will share how God allowed me to go through infertility, financial struggles, pride, and spiritual warfare, all of which He used as building blocks to prepare me for the struggles I would encounter as I learned to be a parent of an Aspie child and to forge through barriers in the education system to get my daughter the help she needed.

Why didn't you tell me?

Sydney's big, blue eyes pierced mine. We were sitting in the living room of our home, and I was reading to her from a social skills book that I had incorporated into our homeschool day.

"Do you remember when your mommy read this book to you, and you learned how to talk to people?"

I was stunned. I had purchased the book along with some others with emotional regulation exercises in my quest to help her to better integrate in the school environment: how to introduce herself, how to wait her turn, how to invite someone to join a game.

Not knowing how to answer her question, I stammered, "Well, I don't have autism, so I guess I learned all of this by watching others. My mom didn't teach me this."

Sydney looked at me incredulously. She couldn't believe that people somehow were born with this ability to decode syntax, tone, and body posture. She shot me a look and bluntly said, "No wonder I didn't understand people and what they meant. Why didn't you tell me a long time ago that I was not normal?"

~

Chapter One
Plan A

On a December evening in 1994, I walked down the aisle in my grandparents' church to marry the love of my life, my childhood sweetheart, Dan Holmes. I had just celebrated my twentieth birthday in October. I had finished high school at sixteen and had graduated college at nineteen, by taking eighteen to twenty-one hours each semester and taking classes during the summer.

Dan and I both wanted to wait a few years before getting pregnant so we could save money for a home and advance our careers before children joined our family. Dan originally wanted four children; I knew I would be happy with two, but we would have time to work that out. I wanted a year's break before pursuing my master's degree, so I began to look for a job. There are few options in the psychology field for a person with only a Bachelor's degree, but I went to the resource center of a local college and lo, and behold, a therapeutic foster-to-adopt home was looking for psychology majors to work with four children. This would be a piece of cake.

Little did I know that working with these four children in the therapeutic group home would afford me the worst cases of abuse and trauma I would ever face. On this uncharted course, I learned skills I thought I would never use outside of this home. The abuse and torture these children had experienced is more gruesome than any horror film ever made. The children were angry, often violent, highly sexualized, and required hyper-vigilance every moment of every day. They were considered too volatile to attend public school, so Home Education Services were sent to educate them. In this position, I learned about high-risk children, 504 plans, Individualized Education Plans (IEP), play therapy, and most important, how to safely do therapeutic holds to protect a child and yourself from physical harm. The children would often self-injure. They would lash out violently toward others, and they were prone to run away and hide.

Hearing these young children's horrific stories and seeing the tremendous wounds they carried emotionally, mentally, and worse, spiritually, was not a piece of cake, after all. It was a very difficult assignment. Working in this sort of environment takes its toll, and being a victim now of the aggressive outbursts and sexual behavior of these children, I experienced what they now referred to as secondary post-traumatic stress disorder (PTSD).

I watched the foster parents fighting for the rights of the children to receive education, therapeutic services from competent therapists, and then defending their own decisions as parents and even their own faith. They struggled with psychiatrists over medicine dosages and tried to explain that the medications didn't work the same in highly traumatized children who had also been diagnosed with multiple personality disorder (now called DID). They traveled across the United States trying to learn from the best in these fields. It was considered an anomaly to have children with multiple personality disorder, or DID, as that had been thought of as an adult's disorder. The foster parents needed expert advice on how to get what they legally needed to help these children.

I saw the toll all of this took on this loving family. I watched how it drained their finances as one parent had to quit work to stay at home twenty-four/seven. I saw how this changed the interactions with their adult children and, soon, their biological grandchildren. Finances were further strained by legal battles to adopt the children and to make up for the lack of services they received. The amount of repair needed to the home, personal belongings, and vehicles after one of the children would react violently or aggressively in an MPD episode was staggering. The emotional stress of simply taking the kids to a store to shop or planning a birthday or holiday party could fill a book.

What stuck with me was that these foster parents celebrated every good day and every success great or small, because they never knew when the next success would be. They treasured every positive moment with the children. I remember thinking, *I hope this never happens to me.* As much as I loved these children and their adoptive family, the stress of working there took its toll. After about fifteen months I resigned and began working on my master's degree. I had learned nothing about DID or PTSD in undergraduate school. This experience, as stressful as it was, gave me invaluable knowledge, skills, and experience, but it also made me a little jaded.

Back in the day (from 1979 to 1999), these high-risk or at-risk kids were referred to by the educational system as "Willie M." children. This special needs category included autistic and mentally challenged children or any child that had violent or aggressive behavior issues that kept them from being in mainstream classrooms. Willie M.'s presented a safety issue for the school, for themselves, for other students, or for the teacher.

I selfishly began dialoguing with God: *Please do not let me have a "Willie M" child. Please, don't let me have an autistic child or a child who is severely challenged physically. There is no way, God, that I could handle an autistic child, or a child that is mentally challenged in any way, or a Down's syndrome child, or any child with extreme behaviors like I saw in the group home.* I never wanted to have to fight the school system like these unfortunate parents had to do for years. That would make me crazy!

As I worked on my graduate degree and licensure, I needed a flexible job, so I could earn a modest income while pursuing my studies. Dan and I had just paid off my undergraduate loans, and he didn't want us to take out any more credit. As a business major, he wanted us to pay for school as I went, so we would not incur further debt. I knew that was a smart decision, so I began to nanny for a set of three siblings. This was what I needed—to be around normal children with everyday, common sense issues. After working as a High-Risk Intervention Specialist in the foster home, these three siblings were, indeed, a piece of cake. The mom was expecting child number four, and when he was born I would care for him also. I had a blast playing "mom" as the nanny to the five-year-old, three-year-old, and the eighteen-month-old. I loved these kids so much I could not imagine loving my own children more. When the baby was born, I enjoyed every second of caring for him. He was a dream baby. I remember crying when I went with the children to get their vaccines and the baby cried. It hurt me to see him sad.

This began to rush my plan to have children. I was now dreaming of my own babies. I could see it now—two boys, maybe a girl, or maybe two girls, if Dan could convince me to have four children. I started to take on more classes, so I could finish my Master's. I wanted to experience the blessing of having children of my own.

In my core group of friends, I was the youngest and each of my friends had at least one child. Some were already planning for their second. The more time Dan and I spent with our friends and their families, the more I wanted my own children. I was ready, I just knew it! We moved from an apartment to our first home to plan for this next phase of life's journey. I was living my own Christian-American dream.

Then, in 1996, my doctor gave me some devastating news. An ectopic pregnancy I'd had awhile back, combined with endometriosis, a retro-vertex uterus, and a shriveled left ovary did not make it look promising for me to have children.

How could this be? I wanted to wail. I was a good Christian girl. I had pretty much done things by the book. Everyone else made having children look so easy. I'd heard many friends and relatives my age make comments like, "Oh, I think I would like a summer baby," or, "I think I would like a fall baby," and no problem, there it was. No problem! Why would I not be able to experience this joy? When you are told that something you desire may not happen, the aching in your heart can be too much to bear.

Suddenly, being around other people's children was painful. I had begun training at a Christian crisis pregnancy center that sought to help young women in unplanned pregnancies gain the resources to choose life for their babies instead of abortion. The ministry supported women who had made the brave, selfless choice of adoption and taught them how to make better lifestyle choices, such as abstinence and relationship choices. So, I was surrounded by pregnant women who, for the most part, did not want to be pregnant. Some of them were very fertile and apparently had no problem getting pregnant, having already had several abortions before they were even twenty years old!

As tragic as their stories were, and as unfortunate as their circumstances must have been to bring them to this point, it felt like God was mocking me. I wanted so desperately to be pregnant and was surrounded by women who were but were often angry and bitter about it. Many were unwed teens, women in abusive relationships, financially desperate women with multiple children already, addicts, and sexually active women who simply used abortion as birth control.

I found myself struggling to find compassion. There were those I still felt merciful toward, those who were pregnant and trying to do the right thing by their babies. My heart and prayers went out to them. However, my sympathy was waning for women having multiple abortions when I longed to just get pregnant once. On the days I worked the front desk or took calls for clinic appointments, I began to see the same names and faces come in. Jealousy and bitterness were taking root in my heart.

Verses like Psalm 127:3-5 became a thorn in my spirit: "Behold, children are a heritage from the Lord. The fruit of the womb is a reward. Like arrows in the hand of the warrior, so are the children of one's youth. Happy is the man who has his quiver full of them. They shall not be ashamed." When pastors preached about the joys of having children on Mother's Day or Father's Day, my heart ached. It was a constant reminder that I must not be blessed.

The church I attended was sometimes referred to as the "the First Church of Fertility" because the nurseries and children's classes were always bursting at the seams. Some people joked, "Be careful of drinking the water there." Sundays became a constant reminder of what I did not have, what I longed for.

None of my friends really understood this agony. The longest any one of them had to wait to get pregnant was nine months. Sometimes I thought maybe I made my friends a little uncomfortable, made them feel as if out of respect for my feelings, they had to hide some of their joy or stories about their children. Only one close friend could truly empathize some as she, too, had been diagnosed with endometriosis. My friends tried very hard to include me, but it was becoming clear I was not like them.

My mom was a great source of strength to me and truly knew my pain. It had taken nearly seven years for her to be able to have me. Her doctor had not given her much hope. She was one of twelve children, and some of her younger siblings were already having children. Although she had grown up in church, she didn't have a personal relationship with the Lord at the time. Yet, she called out to Him, hoping He would intervene and allow her to have a child. She tried a new procedure called wedge incision and, miraculously, was able to conceive. She encouraged me to let the Lord be my strength, that He was my Healer. He was my hope.

Some meaningful but not so helpful Christians tried to throw Scriptures at me, offering little Christian Band-Aid quips like:

"It will happen in God's time."
"Maybe you need to just pray more. Claim those children!"
"Maybe the Lord knows you're not ready for children," or worse, "The Lord knows you shouldn't have children."
"Everything works out for those who love God. Do you love God?"
"Maybe you have sin in your life blocking your prayers."
"Let go, and let God!"

If you have ever been tempted to say these things, let me tell you, they bring little comfort to the one who is suffering. Not only do they not help, they hurt. While the comments are meant to be encouraging, often they bring discouragement and condemnation. Sometimes, it is better simply to listen, to care. And instead of saying, "I will pray for you," maybe pray right then for the Holy Spirit to bring comfort. We do not know the mind of God and why something is being allowed to happen. While some of these sayings have truth, they may be better left for motivational bumper stickers, Facebook quips, and refrigerator magnets. When a person is hurting, trite expressions bring no comfort.

I began to obsess about the story of Hannah in 1 Samuel, hoping to find some ancient secret prayer to kind of "make" God answer my request. Hannah had been infertile, and she cried out to the Lord. He heard her cries, and she bore Samuel. Was there some sort of secret I had missed? Was there a formula in her crying out? How did she persuade God to give her a child? As I studied and studied this story, a verse became troubling to me. First Samuel 1:5: included this phrase: "though the Lord had closed her womb." What? God did this to her on purpose? I began a Bible search of the word *womb*. There were many times God "opened a womb" or "He closed the womb." The thought began to taunt me: *If God is the author of life and He chooses which wombs to open and close, why is He doing this to me?*

It didn't make sense. One day, I just needed to talk to one of the leaders of the ministry about this subject. Why did these women who did not want children keep getting pregnant and having abortions? Why were their wombs opened and mine closed? As we talked, I came to realize I was working with a population that, for the moment, I could not empathize with because of my own struggle. Could my personal issue get in the way of truly ministering to them? The leaders were gracious and understanding. They agreed that because the area of my pain was around pregnancy, talking to pregnant women about unwanted children was not a good environment for me then, but they welcomed me to return when I was ready.

In addition to the emotional pain of infertility, I began to let my feelings skew my image of God. This is not good for a counselor-in-training. I began to see God as unjust, unfair, and uncaring in His dealings with me. Here is a word of caution for all Christians: When we begin to judge God's character by how we feel He answers prayer or what we feel is being done or left undone, we forget that He sees the bigger picture. We begin to limit Him to the present, and we forget He is not limited by our time frame. Simply put, His ways are not our ways. His timing is not always our timing. He is faithful and just, and when our heart, which Jeremiah 17:9 says is deceitful above all things, tries to overrule our mind, things get skewed.

I was saved at age five. I grew up in a Christian home. I had been educated at Christian schools my whole life, but I had missed something in all my spiritual training. I was seeing God as a taker, a punisher, and a withholder, instead of a giver. In my wounding, I could take a verse like James 1:17 that says, "Every good and perfect gift comes from above" and somehow make it a promise for everyone but me. At least I was in good company; Eve did the same thing. She wanted what she thought God was withholding from her, instead of focusing on the paradise around her.

Eve had a perfect life scenario. Years later, we are far removed from the utopia of the Garden of Eden, but it's easy to see how even Christians get a distorted image of God. I had forgotten this simple fact: Being a Christian is not freedom from pain and trials. Christ is the answer, then, of what to do in the pain. He is the direction when we do not know the way and we are off course. The distortion started when Eve doubted God's goodness and His plan for her, and she wanted more. How do we modern Christians get our view skewed?

Well, as Solomon said, "There is nothing new under the sun," (Ecclesiastes 1:9).

Chapter Two
Will You Still Trust?

After a little more than a year of wondering why I couldn't get pregnant and trying formula prayers, on Mother's Day 1997, I laid my desire down at the altar. I called out to the Lord as Hannah did and decided I had to leave it there. My prayer would continue to be: "Lord, if it is your will for me to have children, please heal my body and allow me to get pregnant. If it is not your will, please take this desire and this pain from me." That was it. I needed peace. That day, I left it there in the Lord's hands.

That decision put me in a better place emotionally and spiritually. While it did not make being infertile easier, it did make me feel less discontent. I continued in my studies and working toward my Master's degree. In January 1998, I took a course on campus at Liberty University, and we divided into groups for role-play of counseling activities. We were together from 8:30 a.m. to 5:30 p.m., all week. On the last day of the course, the professor asked us to hear each other's needs and pray for each other. We were to share requests and be transparent. I was in a group of all men, but I mustered up the courage to share my request: "I pray God will heal me, so I can have children."

The first guy to comment was a pastor of ten years. He said that he never prayed because prayer was useless. Because God has pre-ordained the universe and all of our lives, whether I would have children was already decided. To pray about it was nonsense. So, in our moments of transparency, he honestly admitted he would not pray for me.

Well, that was not what I was expecting. As I was repositioning my dropped jaw from that little gem, another group member, Pastor Will from New Jersey, began to share how he and his wife had been through two miscarriages, and he was so sorry for how I was feeling.

I asked, "Isn't God supposed to give us the desires of our heart?" I explained how I had been claiming this verse and trying to use it to sustain me, but it was becoming distressing, instead of encouraging.

Pastor Will took me to Psalm 37:4, "Delight yourself also in the Lord, and He shall give you the desires of your heart" (NKJV). Or as it is said in other verses:

"Then shall you delight yourself in the Lord; and I will cause you to ride on the high hills of the earth" (Isaiah 58:14).
"'He trusts in the Lord,' they say, 'let the Lord rescue him. Let him deliver him, since he delights in him'" (Psalm 22:8).

A light bulb clicked on in my heart. This man was actually a pastor taking this course to be better in his counseling skills. He gently asked me, "If children are not in your future, will you still trust in the Lord? Love the Lord?" What a powerful question that resonated in me!

He went on to explain that in our human relationships, if someone only loved us because of what we provided for them, that would be hurtful. We want people to love us for who we are, not just what we can do for them. He said to pray about the "What if," that is, "What if God does not do this for me as I wish?" Would I still love Him and delight in Him alone? What if I just purposed in myself to delight in Him? My wedding vows came to mind but in reference to God. Could I love Him in "sickness and death, in riches or in poverty, forsaking all others?"

Pastor Will then prayed for me, for my healing, but more that my soul would truly long after God and I would find my delight in Him.

As I sought after Him, I began to search for His face and not His hand. I wish I could remember Pastor Will's last name to thank him for listening to me, showing empathy, asking me a great question, and then praying for me.

January 1998 came to a close. I was finishing up my last intensive class. I had one more class to complete my degree course work. I would simply focus on finishing school and leave the timing of children to God's plan. I would concentrate on my relationship with Him and let Him handle my heart's desire. Finally, my mind was at rest.

As in years past, our pastor had called for a thirty-day fast in January. I had begun the fast with the idea that I was fasting for a pregnancy. Now, after this divine meeting at school, I was fasting for the purpose of getting closer to God and seeking His will for my life and ministry.

In this new quest for peace and God's timing, I stopped doing all the things required for my infertility treatment. I quit counting days, keeping temperatures, tracking parts of my cycle, and timing the frequency of the mechanism required to have a baby. All of that was great, but it was adding to my angst and the it-hasn't-happened-yet-so-it-will-never-happen thought pattern.

For no logical reason, I had this sense that February was going to be a wonderful month. I had the excitement and anticipation of a good change coming. I rationalized that it must be because I was about to start my final class for my Master's and soon would be done with school and the exhaustion of studying.

Then, in March, I began to suspect that I could be pregnant. I didn't tell a soul but my husband, just in case it was a false alarm. Even though an at-home pregnancy test read positive, I wasn't about to get my hopes up. I went to the doctor and had a test, which also read positive. Then, I scheduled myself for a blood test, because I had heard the other tests can give a false-positive.

I was telling no one but Dan without 100 percent certainty. I made a banner on the computer that said, "Dad-to-Be," and put it on his office door. He didn't really react but gave me more of a quizzical response, as if he didn't know how it had happened.

When the blood test came back positive, the next dilemma was who to tell and in what order. Both sets of parents were close to us, and both would want to know first, so we had a dinner and invited both sets. During the dinner prayer, I said: "Thank you, Lord, for the opportunity to have our parents over to dinner to tell them that I am pregnant! Amen."

I opened my eyes to see tears of joy in both moms' eyes. I still wanted to see an ultrasound or hear a heartbeat before we told the entire church body, and this was difficult for our moms. They were ready to tell the world about the first grandchild.

I was officially confirmed March 12, 1998. The doctor said I was in good health, and everything looked good. She gave me a due date of November 4. As it turns out, we were having a youth reunion party March 14 for our former youth group friends, and we made the big announcement then. There was much rejoicing. The news was out: We were having a baby!

Overall, I had a great pregnancy with very little sickness. As long as Dan had crackers and ginger ale waiting for me at the bedside before I got out of bed, it was all good. I was convinced I was going to have a boy, you know, like Hannah. I liked the names Samuel and Alexander, so I thought maybe we'd use Samuel Alexander, but Dan's middle name is Christopher, so maybe Samuel Christopher.

Seeing the baby on the ultrasound was amazing. It was breathtaking to see it, to know it was real, and to see that it looked healthy. The little stinker was a bit obstinate and stubborn during this ultrasound, though. The technician had scheduled twenty minutes for our ultrasound, and the baby either had its hand over the private area, or it turned away, as if to keep the secret a mystery until November. Finally, at minute 18.5, she revealed herself to us for a few seconds. Then, she was done and no longer wished to be viewed. Of course, I thought she was already beautiful, and, obviously, trying to figure out a boy's name was no longer an issue.

At first, I have to say I was shocked to think I was having a girl. As I was dressing and preparing to leave the office to return to work that day, I remembered to delight in the Lord. I remembered that God is fond of surprise gifts. Surprise, it's a girl! I would have to return all the boy clothes I had already bought.

What to name her? We agreed that we wanted a name no female on either side of the family had, so neither side could possibly be offended. I wanted Danielle, but Dan would not have it.

He said, "The family will call her 'Little Danny' and that would be annoying."

I countered, "So, what about an 'S' name, since my name starts with S. ... Samantha? Sydney?" Sydney was a unique name, so we went with Sydney. After all, another desire of my heart was to go to Australia.

The middle name was easy. As a young girl, I had decided if I ever had a girl, she would have the middle name Christine. When I was about ten or eleven years old, there was a television show with an actress named Khrstyne. I thought the spelling looked very cool, and my middle name was Christine, so I figured it would be neat that when I grew up, my daughter would have my name spelled a different way. When I ran in the kitchen to share this news with my mom, she said: "Did you know my middle name and your grandmother's name is also Christine? See how the word *Christ* is in the spelling? I kind of look at it like having Christine spelled this way as a middle name is a reminder to keep Christ in the middle of your life." Hmmm, I liked that. Christine it would be.

We went to work on preparing the nursery for Sydney Christine Holmes. The schoolwork part of my degree was done, and I secured a new nanny job scheduled around my counseling intern hours. The two little girls were a dream. They were so excited that I was having a girl and so excited as I got bigger and bigger, meaning the time was passing and they would get to hold her.

The nursery was beautiful. I had so much fun helping with what little I could do. My mother-in-law, Brenda, and my best friend, Janet, went to work painting. I had decided on Winnie the Pooh, and I rescued some Pooh and Friends that Janet had made for the church nursery but that were no longer being used. A church friend hand made some beautiful shelves, which are still hanging in Sydney's current room in his memory.

Some days, I would sit in the finished room, rocking in the rocking chair, just dreaming about holding and rocking Sydney. I imagined all the wonderful things that would happen in this room: the games we would play, the stories we would read. September seemed to go by so slowly. Would November ever get here? I decided to write Sydney a letter in the scrapbook I had already started for her. I was an avid scrapbook-er, and it would be great to actually scrapbook with my friends, talk about our kids, and not feel awkward, anymore. It took me awhile to put my thoughts into words in that tiny, little space in the scrapbook, but I wrote:

"Mommy and Daddy met at [church] in 1984. Back then

our church was a small chapel building that is no longer around. Mommy knew Daddy was the one for her, but Daddy wasn't so sure. Then again, he was twelve and Mommy was ten. We dated off and on and eventually became the best of friends. We began dating February of 1991. ... We were engaged on July 23, 1993. We were married at my grandparents' church, St. Luke's Lutheran Church, on December 17, 1994. Mommy and Daddy are very involved in our church because we love the Lord. We are already praying for you that you will grow up and love the Lord with all of your heart.

"In 1996, we began praying for a baby. The doctor told Mommy there would be problems having a baby, but Mommy and Daddy believed God would hear our prayers. It was a difficult time to just trust and believe. God has perfect timing and He wanted to give us the most perfect gift—He wanted us to have YOU. ... Mommy and Daddy won't be perfect, but we promise to always love you and follow God's voice and as best as possible to do what is best for you. Daddy and Mommy's love for Jesus brought us together, and we hope to illustrate that unconditional love to you. We love you!"

My birthday had come and gone, and now I was ready for November. Secretly, I hoped Sydney would also be born in October. On October 7, I penned another letter to her that said, in part:

"I am so excited and am just waiting to meet you. I wonder who you will look like? Whose personality might you have? ... I can't wait to be involved with you at church or school plays. Maybe you will be a cheerleader or gymnast or our little dancer. Whoever you are, and whatever you are like, Mommy will always love you. ... I cannot wait to take you places and make our own memories ... Love, Mommy."

On October 29, I went in for my usual appointment. I was 39 weeks. The doctor got this concerned look on his face and asked, "Did you know you were having contractions?" He added, "With each contraction, the baby's heart decelerates. I would feel better if

28

you went on to the hospital."

Wait? For real? Like, it's time?

He said, "I'm calling the hospital to tell them you will be there soon. You're going to meet that baby today, hopefully."

Sydney was born later that night—well, technically, in the morning, at 1:07, October 30, 1998. There aren't even words to describe what it felt like to hold her and feel God's answer to prayers in such a tangible way. It was emotionally overwhelming.

I wish I could say I never doubted the Lord's faithfulness or goodness to me ever again, but, alas, I cannot. I still held on to the prayer I prayed throughout the pregnancy, "Please, God, don't let her have autism or be mentally challenged."

I had become fearful of having a child with a life-altering condition. Memories of the therapeutic foster home and the sacrifices the family made for those special needs children flooded my mind. I remembered how they fought the powers that be for therapeutic services and education, and the stress it created. That scared me. There obviously was still a lack of trust in God, and I still wanted total control of my life, career, and family.

Chapter Three
Divine Intervention

I had begun working hours for licensure, and during this time, I was interning at a great counseling center that worked around my schedule and even allowed me to bring the baby on campus, when necessary. I also was still a nanny for the two girls. They adored Sydney, and I was allowed to bring her to work there, too.

Dan's job as a computer programmer was going well. I was completing my hours for licensure at a rapid pace. My mom and mom-in-law were available to help with Sydney, if I was in a pinch. Sydney was a fabulous baby. She was good-natured and flexible. She ate and slept on schedule and was everything you could ask for in a baby. Things at church were at a good place. I had everything my heart desired. I was thankful my trial was over, and finally everything was now going to go according to plan.

Now, if anyone reading this does not believe in a real enemy, a real Satan, I am here to tell you he is real, and his goal is, as Scripture says, "to steal, kill, and destroy" (John 10:10). When God blesses you with something, your enemy wants you to be fearful, doubtful, or discouraged, so you will take your eyes off of God.

For no reason that I could fathom, I began to have feelings of sadness. I had nothing to be sad or depressed about, yet I had this weird feeling that I could not explain. I pulled out my Diagnostic Statistical Manual (DSM-IV) to check the symptoms for clinical depression and anxiety. I asked others who knew me if I seemed depressed. No one felt I showed the clinical signs, but I was still perplexed, so I went to a pastor for prayer and counsel.

As we discussed the issue and prayed, he helped me see I was carrying false guilt. See, some of my closest friends were in the midst of major struggles. One was having financial challenges, one was having issues with her in-laws, and one couple had to move back in with parents. Because things were not going well my friends' lives, I felt guilty that things were going so well for me.

I looked up false guilt. It was a kind of survivor's guilt. When two people are in an accident and one dies, the survivor can have conflicted feelings—guilt for surviving, coupled with happiness for surviving.

I mention this as part of my story because I have now been counseling with Christians seventeen to nineteen years, and I find this to be a common issue. Please remember, as I had to, that guilt and condemnation do not come from our Heavenly Father:

> "Come to me, all you who are weary and burdened, and I will give you rest," Jesus says in Matthew 11:28.
> "God has not given us a spirit of fear, but of power and of love and of a sound mind" (2 Timothy 1:7, NKJV).
> "Therefore there is now no condemnation for those who are in Christ Jesus" (Romans 8:1).
> "Casting all your cares upon Him, for He cares for you" (1 Peter 5:7).

These feelings of guilt and condemnation are meant to steal joy and life from you. They are meant to paralyze you and keep you from living an active Christian life. We know these feelings are not from God, so who are they from? They are from the one called "the accuser of the brethren" in Revelation 12:10. Our enemy is the inventor of the game, "Devil's Advocate." When things are not going well, he wants you to doubt God and His faithfulness. He wants you to blame God and see Him as the adversary. When things are going well and you are moving forward, he wants you to think you have done this on your own, or to be fearful for the "other shoe to drop," so you do not enjoy the blessing. He will tell you that you don't deserve to be happy.

Keep these Scriptures in mind:

"Be transformed by the renewing of your mind" (Romans 12:2, NKJV).

"For our struggle is not against flesh and blood, but against the rulers, against the authorities, against the powers of this dark world and against the spiritual forces of evil in the heavenly realms" (Ephesians 6:12).

"For the flesh desires what is contrary to the Spirit, and the Spirit what is contrary to the flesh. They are in conflict with each other, so that you are not to do whatever you want" (Galatians 5:17).

The trials of infertility and sadness did not prepare me for every hardship I would ever face, but they did strengthen me for the set of trials immediately ahead. Just like seasons change in nature, seasons change in life, and each one brings about a different kind of fruit. Or, they expose areas without fruit. Study the children of Israel, because thousands of years later, we believers are no different. When things are good and plentiful, it is easy to stray from the faith and become self-reliant. It is in seasons of struggle that we learn who really is in control, and then we call out to Him for help in those times of stress and sorrow.

In 1999, our church body went through a traumatic moral failure. It was a year of heartache for us. As we were one of the remaining founding families of the church, the hurt was great. Much of that year centered around healing from that ordeal. But life moved on, and, having come through that year with a few spiritual and emotional scars, I enjoyed my beautiful, little girl and wondered how family life could be any better. I had a wonderful husband who was faithful to me and loved me, a beautiful and healthy baby girl, and a supportive family. The church would heal, and I was about to begin my own private practice. I was on cloud nine, thinking I was in a season that would linger forever.

After all, Christians are not called to suffer like the world, right? If you are just spiritual enough and pray enough, all will go well. I don't know who started that rumor in the Body of Christ, but I think we've forgotten John 16:33, "In this world you will have trouble. But take heart! I have overcome the world."

I thought I was so much stronger in my faith as a result of my struggle with infertility, but there were so many more lessons to learn.

In the fall of 2000, we signed a contract to build a new home. The home would be twice the size of the little house we were living in at the time. The floor plan had all the extras—a spa tub, front porch, upgraded floors and cabinets, and the best master suite closet I had seen in a house plan we could afford. I loved it!

We put our house on the market and had immediate interest. The builder was wonderful; he kept giving us extensions to sell our home. We thought this was the Lord working things out on our behalf.

However, by April 2001, it was evident that we were not meant to sell our home. We had many prospective buyers, but their finances would fall through, or they had to wait until they could sell their current home or farmland.

The builder released us from the contract and returned our money. The new house sold on April 15, within seventy-two hours of being put on the market. It was no longer my dream house. Someone else would live in it.

I was devastated. I had already picked out so many things that fit my personal taste. Why wouldn't God sell our house? Why wouldn't He let me have this piece of happiness? Later on in the year, I would document that the fact that we did not move was God's protection.

We had no way of knowing that the manufacturing economy was shifting overseas and how greatly this would hurt the company my husband was working for at the time. We were counting on his yearly salary increase to be able to afford the new house payment, but that increase didn't happen. In fact, we wouldn't get an annual cost of living raise for six more years! We would have been in trouble within six to nine months of living in that new home.

God knew the economy was changing. He knew our pay was not going to cover the mortgage. Although I had been devastated when God said no, it was for my own good. God answered our prayer with protection, instead of giving me what I wanted. Not only did we not get the cost of living raise, but our overall income also fell by 30 percent within six months. The house I was calling my dream home would have turned into a nightmare.

After watching the house sell on April 15, I had this strange feeling that this date would be significant to me in the future. It would have greater meaning than just another tax day or as the day my dream house sold.

One reason I had wanted a bigger home was because I wanted more children. The previous summer, I had really begun to yearn for a second child. That June, I had seen the doctor about medical options to help me conceive and maintain a pregnancy. I was not prepared for what she would say that day.

I had been in a lot of pain for a long time but had no idea why. The doctor began to run various tests, including a screening for cancer. Based on the preliminary tests, she said the issues contributing to my infertility—endometriosis, a retroverted uterus, and a shriveled left ovary—had progressed and were far worse than the first time I had tried to get pregnant. We would have to wait and see. Her face seemed to communicate concern and doubt.

But because of God's faithfulness in allowing me to get pregnant with Sydney, I knew He could intervene and give us a second child, despite the obstacles. I knew it would not be easy to wait on Him, but I knew it was possible in His timing to have another child.

The doctor felt that I wouldn't be able to have any more children, in her words, "without Divine intervention." I didn't have cancer, but there was too much scarring, other disease, and syndromes involved for the medical community to conceive that another child was possible. They had told me Sydney's conception would be slim, but this report said, "not medically possible." So, I had begun fertility treatments while we were still trying to sell the house.

There was medicine to take, an excessive number of trips to the doctor for scans and hormone level checks, and planning for the proper timing of conception, in addition to the high costs of this treatment. It was terrible. All of the poking and prodding left me feeling like a lab rat. The act that was meant to bring intimacy between two married people had become rote work in an effort to achieve conception. Every month the anticipation of success was met with disappointment and discouragement. So, while dealing with this medical news and then losing out on the new home, I was again spiraling into the "Why Me? blues."

In late July, the doctor said she could not see that the treatments were working, so she wanted to do a laparoscopy for further exploration of the problem. We scheduled it for September 10, 2001. I kept hoping that God would use the fertility treatments as a way to bring about the miracle. We kept praying that God would heal me so I could have another child, but the actual scheduling of the procedure made me lose hope of that ever happening. I left the doctor that day feeling discouraged and confused.

I knew that God could do the impossible, but would He do the impossible for me? Could I ask Him for another miracle? I mean, after all, I did have one healthy child. Was I being greedy?

I got on my cellphone when I left the doctor's office that day and began to call everyone I could think of to listen to me vent on the subject. I called my husband, my mom, my closest friend, my mom-in-law, other friends, and even pastoral staff. Every line was busy! No one was answering the phone. I was so frustrated.

I sat back and turned on the radio full blast, only to hear Nicole C. Mullen singing, "When I Call on Jesus". The chorus echoed through the car:

"When I call on Jesus, all things are possible.
I can mount on wings of eagles and soar.
When I call on Jesus, mountains are gonna fall
'cause He'll move Heaven and earth to come rescue me
when I call."

Wow! The one who could truly help me and hear my cries was the last person I thought of calling on in my distress. So I called out to Him while driving the twenty miles home that day. Was it His will for me to have another child? Was this protection again? After all, our finances were not in good shape, and our income was down 30 percent. I needed guidance and reassurance, but to have another child would require an even bigger miracle than the first pregnancy did! Isn't it funny how the human mind reasons how something is bigger for God to do? Like thinking, *Could God pull off something bigger that is considered impossible?* We forget in our times of distress what Luke 1:37 says: "For nothing is impossible with God."

Let's see, what was the lesson I learned when I was praying to get pregnant the first time? Seek God's face and not just His hand. Continue to trust and not get angry with Him. Keep my eyes on Him, no matter what I see happening in the circumstances. This was going to require some more faith on my part.

Chapter Four

Pruning and Preparation

As we began this second stage of trials and difficulties, Dan suggested that I make a new scrapbook. I was an avid scrapbook-er, and he had made a very astute observation about my craft: My scrapbooks contained only happy memories.

"How would our children know what God had brought us through if they only saw happy, positive, fairytale pictures in these books?" he asked.

During this time, we were reading Bruce Wilkinson's *Secrets of the Vine*, which is a study of John 15. We prayed, read Scriptures, and wondered, *Why are these things happening to us?* We went through the checklist we had been given by older, more mature believers: Was there sin in our lives? Were we tithing? Were we doubting? Did we harbor unforgiveness? We found the answers in John 15.

The study led to me begin a scrapbook called, "Abiding in the Vine." Here, we would document hard times and then journal or discuss how the situation was resolved.

It was in this time that we discovered we were not being punished but pruned. John 15:1-2 says, "I am the true vine, and my Father is the gardener. He cuts off every branch that bears no fruit, while every branch that does bear fruit He prunes."

After many months, we came to realize that this time of pruning was also a time of preparing. But for what, we were not sure. Still, we knew it was for something bigger than us, something that would require us to rely on God. In response, I penned these words: "This album is our effort to record things we are learning, so that we may remember God's providence, protection, and times of pruning. As the Israelites were instructed to teach their children and their children's children the ways of God, we hope this album will remind us and future generations of the promises and blessings of our God."

After our study of John 15, we cried out for answers to these hardships. We learned that "abiding in the vine" meant there would be more than one season of pruning, and in seasons of pruning there are varying degrees of harvest and abundance. What is allowed will be in God's timing. We get caught up in the fact that blessings are financial, but there are so many other aspects of God's blessings. In 2001, we began to record sorrows, hardships, and blessings and the lessons that followed.

For me, this book is a reminder not to be distracted and distraught in times of pruning. We noted events that were struggles, and then we documented the answers to these trials with a photo or some other piece of memorabilia.

Dan did not struggle in the hard times nearly as much as I did. I am blessed to have a spouse who is such a great a prayer warrior. He had enough faith for the both us. He entered a time of fasting and praying for my physical healing and for us to have a second child. It was a regular part of his week to take a certain time of the day to pray for this specific need. He and two fellow workers formed a prayer group to fast and pray for each other's needs—the Body of Christ in action! These three men united in prayer to hold up their families.

Perhaps for this reason, Dan was a little discouraged at first when I told him I had scheduled the exploratory surgery for September. He felt as if maybe I was giving up and not allowing God to do His work in me. He was praying that the surgery would not be necessary. Nevertheless, he continued to pray and support me in my decision.

I will never forget what happened that August when a special speaker came for a Sunday night service at our church. When I heard the announcement on Sunday morning that the evening service would have a focus on healing, I was not excited. I had been praying for a second pregnancy for a year, and my husband and his prayer group had been praying intensely, so why would one more prayer service really matter? I didn't want to go up to the altar one more time for this request only to return upset, frustrated, hurt, or even angry. After all, the surgery was planned. I had given God His chance to intervene, and He had chosen not to.

But we went to the evening service, anyway. The speaker began to pray and call out specific needs, signaling for people with those needs to come down for prayer. Surely, he would not call out infertility, an issue that is so personal. If he named that need specifically, my friends and family would expect that I would want to have prayer for this—again. I would then have to force myself to go down, get my hopes up, and possibly be disappointed. Again.

See, counselors can pray with fervor and believe for you to hear from God or to be touched by God. We can have faith that can move a mountain for you but not always necessarily for ourselves. I have never doubted God could and would work a miracle for a client or someone I was praying with at the altar. But, often, I struggled for faith for my own situations, needs, and issues.

As I feared, the speaker said he wanted to pray for someone who wanted to have a baby. Well, there were many women there with endometriosis and fertility issues, so maybe I could sit this one out.

Women began to move toward the altar, but the speaker paused and said, "Wait! This is not prayer for a first child, but for a second child. This is more about completing a family, instead of starting a family."

The ladies sat down. Great! That was me. I watched, hoping someone else was going to get up. No one was stirring, just looking around to see who was supposed to go up. I sighed, tugged on my husband's sleeve and said, "Alright, let's get this over with, I guess."

The pastor sensed my lack of faith and desire to be at the altar praying, yet, he encouraged me to pray. He reminded me that things take place in the Lord's timing, so that the result will glorify Him. He prayed for us. As the timeline of events unfolded, I did conceive that very week. Somehow, I knew the day it happened it was for real and I was pregnant, with no real proof or evidence. It was just an inner knowing.

I called my doctor to set up a prenatal appointment. She was not as excited as I was. She said conceiving was only one-fourth of the battle. As great as it was that I had conceived, she was not convinced I would be able to maintain the pregnancy. She did not cancel the exploratory surgery or give me a due date; she simply wrote a prescription for a medicine that would help me maintain the pregnancy. I almost let myself get discouraged, but I knew this was for real and God had worked a miracle. This time I chose to trust and believe and try to walk by faith and not by sight or by knowledge of the odds against me.

While all of this was going on, I was preparing for my first trip as a counselor to the American Association of Christian Counselors World Conference in Nashville, Tennessee. When I got to the conference, I noticed a woman crying, and I went over to minister to her. I simply listened and offered some advice.

She found me later that week to say she was doing better and thanked me for listening. She wanted to do something for me but said she had nothing to offer. She mentioned that she had a small ministry, but it didn't apply to me. I asked what the ministry was.

She answered, "I feel led to pray for high-risk pregnancies. I pray every day until the baby arrives."

My eyes lit up. I told her about my situation, and she committed to pray for my pregnancy every day. We exchanged emails, and she periodically emailed to check if I needed a specific prayer. Another miracle had happened in front of my eyes!

At my next appointment, the doctor decided to check for a heartbeat using ultrasound. Waiting for that sound was intense, but after a while, she found it. She declared the pregnancy viable. Praise God! The surgery would be canceled.

My doctor still was uncertain that I would go full-term, and she cautioned against getting set on a due date. When she left to get the nurse, I got the little tool they use to set the due date and figured out that it would be May 4, 2002. When she returned, we had a serious discussion about high-risk pregnancies. If I made it past the first trimester, there was at least hope. I would be watched closely and would need multiple ultrasounds. But all I chose to hear was, "The baby is alive, and the surgery will be canceled."

Well, this did indeed turn out to be a high-risk pregnancy, full of issues and complications. I developed an allergy to the compounded medication I was taking to sustain the pregnancy. My wonderful doctor was pregnant herself and had to go on maternity leave. The interim doctor was less than my favorite, to say it nicely. He nonchalantly prescribed an oral medication for me without discussing my chart or answering any questions. His demeanor indicated that it was no big deal, many people miscarry, so we'll see what happens. He was not nearly as personal and caring as my regular doctor.

He must not have read my chart or noticed that this was considered a high-risk pregnancy. He said my insurance wouldn't cover any more ultrasounds, so he didn't see the need to do one. I told him what my regular doctor had said, that not only was I high risk, but due to taking fertility drugs months prior, there was a risk for multiples. Also, the insurance *would* pay for an ultrasound at fifteen weeks, if there was a medical reason. Still, he wouldn't budge.

I had returned to volunteering at a crisis pregnancy center in a different county. One day, I was teaching a class on sexual abuse, and I told the coordinator about my dilemma. As it turned out, an ultrasound machine had just been donated to the center, and they had a technician who would volunteer to use the machine to help clients see their baby. The hope was that once the clients could see a living baby in their womb, they would make a choice not to terminate the pregnancy.

However, the center was in a dilemma because they could not practice using the ultrasound on a client. They were holding a fundraiser and hoped to have someone pregnant volunteer, so they could demonstrate to the participants how this technology could be helpful to the ministry. Many of the center's volunteers and supporters were older and had not had ultrasounds during their pregnancies. I volunteered, and the ladies coming to the fundraiser would see my baby on the ultrasound, and so would I—for the first time.

I had researched the new medication my doctor had prescribed and was very concerned about one of the precautions. The packaging said it could cause cleft pallet or other mouth and face deformities. I stopped taking it without telling the doctor, but I feared that my baby was still in danger of birth defects because of the length of time I had taken the drug. I was condemning myself for taking this medication without researching it first and had this secret fear and obsessive thoughts about the drug.

When I told my doctor that I was volunteering for an ultrasound since he wouldn't perform one, he decided he should be the first to see an ultrasound, after all. I didn't get a very long view of the baby. The doctor just wanted to see a heartbeat, check for four chambers in the heart, and count the fingers and toes. It was not like the nice, relaxed, first ultrasound I had with Sydney, but at least I learned that the baby was a girl.

At the fundraiser dinner, I was so excited to share what *life* looked like in the womb. I had some time to watch this little girl on the monitor and get excited about meeting her in the spring. I still had that secret fear about cleft pallet, so I was delighted when, out of the blue, the technician said, "I want to see if the machine could detect cleft pallet. Is that OK?" Yes!

After a moment, she looked around and said with a smile that the baby did not have cleft pallet. However, when everyone left the room, she said she had seen something else and wanted to look closer. She took some pictures, so I could show my doctor. I had *placenta previa*, she said, and my doctor needed to know this ASAP.

I took the pictures to the doctor, but he said, "Techs who work at those types of places are not qualified to make such a diagnosis. She must have been looking at the pictures upside down. There's nothing to worry about here." He tossed the pictures in the file without really looking at them. I wasn't reassured and scheduled my next appointment with a different doctor.

Our beautiful Sydney was now in preschool. One day, the preschool had a pre-screening for vision. I wasn't expecting to get a slip of paper suggesting Sydney needed further testing on her vision, so when she came home with one, I thought it was a little dramatic. She could see just fine. She had this same pre-test before, and it also had come back showing concern, but I had never seen her struggle to see anything. Besides, our insurance didn't cover vision, and I wasn't about to spend 200 dollars we didn't have on an exam that seemed unnecessary.

But Prevent Blindness North Carolina was tenacious. They kept calling to ask if I had followed up. I tried to explain that we couldn't afford a vision exam, as it was not covered by insurance. The organization was so insistent that they found an eye doctor willing to do the exam for free. As it turned out, Sydney had severe amblyopia in her left eye, meaning the vision in one eye is reduced because the eye and the brain are not working together properly. The eye itself looks normal, but it is not fully functioning because the brain is favoring the other eye. Sometimes, this condition is called *lazy eye*. Sydney had learned to use her right eye because of the lack of vision in her left. Now that she had a medical diagnosis, she could be covered by medical insurance. We had to start patching her eye. This became a two- to three-year process of torture for both of us.

Sydney hated that patch and refused to wear it. This is when I first began to see her sensory issues, but sensory integration disorder (SID) was not commonly spoken about back then. Worse yet, these patches were one dollar each. We tried every brand of patch on the market, but within minutes, she would pull the patch off. I was not very long-suffering because of the cost compounded by our lack of funds. Every day, it was a struggle to get her to wear the patch and another stressor added to an already stressful pregnancy and an already stretched budget.

In January 2002, I had the scare of my life. "Erica" was about six months in utero. I was at the dentist's office getting my teeth cleaned when I started bleeding and cramping. I called the doctor, who said to go to the hospital, immediately. I was terrified. Well, as luck would have it, the doctor on call was the one I did not like. He did an ultrasound to make sure that I had enough fluid and that my water was not leaking. And, guess what: The ultrasound showed placenta previa. He didn't believe me before, so he hadn't documented it on my chart. So, the bleeding was a result of the placenta issue, and he said to be on the safe side, I needed to get more rest.

In February, after slowing my schedule down and being on bed rest more, I had gained a lot of weight. I was miserable, but I rested like the doctor said. One morning, as I was getting ready to go to church, I felt liquid running down my legs. I thought maybe I was having an embarrassing moment and went to the bathroom to check, but it was not that.

I called the doctor, and he said to lie down and rest. If I felt any cramping, I was to go to the hospital. I did start cramping, and it was getting worse. Our church was on the route to the hospital, so we dropped Sydney off with her grandparents and then headed to the hospital.

I was scared. This was not blood; it was a sticky liquid, and the baby was only six months or so along. If my water was leaking and I would be giving birth today, it was way too early.

We arrived at the hospital, and more ultrasounds were ordered. Another doctor was on call, thankfully, but the placenta previa still hadn't been documented. The attending doctor was stumped until I mentioned it, and he then said, "Oh, that explains it!" His orders:

Quit work, shut down my counseling practice for a while, and rest.

I do not rest well. I certainly could not stay in bed for the next two or three months. I am a doer. I accomplish things, and I multi-task. Resting is a foreign concept. Besides that, I had a three-year-old who got out of pre-school at two o'clock each day, and she needed to be picked up. After school, she wanted to play and be entertained. I joined an indoor play area where I could lie on a bench and she could play for two or three hours. I tried to do phone counseling while lying down at the play place. This was most difficult.

Things were not going as planned. There was so much to prepare for the baby, and I couldn't do it. I've always been fiercely independent, like I imagine a horse running free in the Old West times. Accepting help, much less asking for it, was another foreign concept. I had to add a new behavior to my toolbox, and it was very humbling.

At this point, not only was I not bringing in any income, but Dan's place of employment wasn't doing well, either. In fact, they were about to lay off several employees. Fear began to take over. What if he was laid off? Our insurance was through his job. The company used to pay our portion of insurance, but when it fell on hard times, we had to pick up the $500 a month. Dan hadn't received a cost of living raise in two years, and now, with only one income, we had this monthly bill and a baby on the way. This was scary, and I had no control. Where was my faith? Again, like those Israelites, I couldn't see God working, so I assumed He wasn't.

To recap, the doctor had confirmed that this pregnancy and conception were indeed miraculous. God put a woman in my life who committed to pray for me every day of my pregnancy. I got the diagnosis of placenta previa as a result of volunteering at a crisis pregnancy ministry. I had survived two major scares. And, yet, with all of this, I still lacked faith. I was scared about the finances and insurance and job security.

Going back to the story of the Israelites, they were only content when they saw miracles and got what they wanted. When I studied this story as a child, it always appalled me. I thought, I would never do that! I mean, Pharaoh let them go. And despite the plagues, the Passover angel, the Red Sea, and the food God kept providing, they kept doubting Him! I would say to them in my mind: "Time and again, God proves Himself to you, and you are all singing Janet

Jackson's song, 'What Have You Done for Me, Lately?'" As a child I just did not understand these faithless Israelites. Why couldn't they just trust God? They were His chosen people.

And now, even though I continued to see God intervene in my own life, I was also continuing to wonder, *Will He intervene?* This pregnancy was certainly not the first time I had seen God do a miracle. I had seen the miraculous most of my life, but still I struggled with thoughts like: *Is God really going to pull this off for me? What if I lose the baby here at seven months? I would be devastated and then all those other miracles really would not matter. What if that medication I took caused other deformities? Then it would be my fault. What if my husband faced another pay cut or had to get a second job?*

What if? What if? What if?

My husband's faith never moved or wavered. Sometimes that was reassuring, and sometimes it was annoying! He stayed positive and never showed any worry. Anytime I postulated a "what if" question, he responded that God would take care of it, and He would provide and protect. That should have encouraged me, but at times it made me wonder if he was just dismissing me and not living in reality. I began calling him "Pollyanna" because he always had a positive answer to anything I said.

How had I become like the children of Israel? Again, I was seeking His hand and not His face. I wanted his gifts and presents, but I was not concerned with His presence.

I didn't have peace until Erica was born on April 15. Does that date sound familiar? I remembered that uncanny feeling I'd had the year before when my house had been sold to someone else on April 15. Erica was due May 4, and we were 100 percent sure of the conception time due to all the ultrasounds at the beginning of the pregnancy. Erica came early, yet she weighed eight pounds and 1.4 ounces. She was beautiful and healthy. Dan still had his job, and we had insurance.

Erica was unable to suck at first, so for a week she had to be fed by syringe, but here she was, my living miracle. I reflected on this in my "Abiding in the Vine" scrapbook:

"On April 15, 2001, I was devastated because of the loss of a dream, my home. Yet, later, God's protection is revealed when the economy changed. At that time, I felt like God was taking from me and saying, 'No!' for no reason. I had doubted that He wanted good things for me.

"Later, when I saw His protection, I was grateful. Hindsight is always twenty-twenty. God did have our back. I thought that house was the secret desire of my heart, but God had something better. He wanted to give me the greater desire of my heart—a second baby!

"I got pregnant and said, 'Oh no! What are we gonna do?' when all of the hardships came with the miracle. But on April 15, 2002, a healthy baby girl was born. Finances were tight, but the job was intact. Life was tough, but God did provide!"

Another miracle: One month before Erica was born, the placenta moved and reattached itself to the top of the uterus, instead of blocking the cervix. God did that! The doctor said, "Then you must have never had placenta previa because that's not medically possible." When I reminded him of the ultrasound pictures, he said it must have been someone else's ultrasound because that was impossible.

Erica had also gotten stuck in a breech position, and we were concerned they might have to do a C-section. Two weeks before she was born, she moved into perfect position on her own.

But the bigger miracle, even greater than Erica's actual birth, was that God did not heal my endometriosis and other issues in order for me to conceive. I had four different conditions, and I still carried a baby, despite a negative prognosis from the doctors.

Because I still had the conditions, I still needed that laparoscopy in 2002. My old friends worry and doubt tried to take hold of me, but I didn't murmur and complain to God this time. I did not doubt Him, but I did not completely trust Him, either.

When I had the procedure the doctor reported that the endometriosis was much more severe than she had thought. She believed I had adenomyosis as well, which defined by the Mayo Clinic is "where the endometrial tissue, which normally lines the uterus, exists within and grows into the muscular wall of the uterus." The doctor said the scarring in my uterus was so severe, she had no idea how I carried Erica to term. She said, "I repeat, you had Divine intervention."

So, throughout the whole process of Erica's conception and birth, God was there, intervening on my behalf despite my murmuring and lack of trust. *Take that, children of Israel!* I thought. *I will never murmur again. I have seen the greatest miracle happen in me and through me, and I will never doubt God again.*

I had overcome, and I was ahead of those Hebrew children now. I was going to be like Moses and keep seeking His presence, not His hand.

At least, that was my intention.

Chapter Five
I'm No Superwoman

It was awesome to see God intervene in my health issues and bring about the birth of our second beautiful daughter, Erica. However, our finances were now getting worse, with another mouth to feed and another body to diaper and clothe! By December, we couldn't afford to get diapers, formula, or other food items. Erica needed a winter coat. Our anniversary was approaching, and we couldn't afford to celebrate. In fact, we had not had a date night or gone out as a couple since I was put on bed rest before Erica was born. What to do?

I photographed the empty refrigerator, freezer, and pantry and put the pictures in the scrapbook. We prayed, and I broke down and called the church to ask for food from the food pantry.

There wasn't much in the food pantry because people really need the church's assistance during the holidays. The pastor I had called happened to live near us, and he said he would bring what they had. He said the church would put in a fifty-dollar gift card for the grocery store. Since my mom and mom-in-law both worked at the church, I wanted him to keep this confidential. It was hard enough to ask for help, but this was embarrassing. The fewer people who knew about this, the better. My pride was welling up. This wasn't supposed to happen to me, a good tither.

It appears God felt my pride was an issue and that He needed to break it down a notch. The pastor said he would drop the box off on my front porch on his way home that evening. Because of the gift card inside, he called Dan later to make sure we had received it.

I went to the front porch. It was not there! Really, who would take my food? *Oh no*, I thought, *maybe he left it on the wrong porch*. I had to do the unthinkable: Go ask my neighbors if they had a mysterious box of food on their porch. Surely, they would not ask why, right? I was mortified. My embarrassment was growing, but we needed the food. I started with my closest neighbor.

She said, "You know, my neighbor was wondering why a box of food was left on her porch. Let's go see if she's home." She offered to go with me. Oh, dear! Her neighbor had it. The front of her house resembled mine, so the pastor had made an honest mistake. The numbers on the houses were not in an order that made sense to anyone except those of us who lived on that country road.

I thanked the woman for the box and thought I could get away without an explanation. However, one of the ladies asked why I had that box of food. Drat! I had to confess that money was tight, the pantry and fridge were bare, and our church was helping us. Both women assured me I could have asked them for help, but I am "Stephanie the Independent," so that wasn't an option. I admitted my embarrassment and told them I had a hard enough time asking my own church of twenty years for food. I at least felt that because we had tithed all of our lives, I could ask for the food without too much guilt. I thanked them for caring and sheepishly took my box home.

In the mail that very week, we received fifty dollars from Dan's grandmother in Florida. She said it was an early Christmas gift. Dan's parents' neighbors sent us a fifty-dollar gift card to the local baby stuff store. They said they usually don't send that large of a gift, but they felt bad for taking so long to get us a gift when the baby was born in April that they wanted to make up for it. So, our immediate need for food was met. Erica got a winter coat and some other baby supplies we needed. The early gift from grandma helped us finish buying what we needed to re-stock the pantry.

That same week, we got a call from a timeshare place (one of those three-day, three-night deals to hear a presentation). You may hate those calls, but we loved the free vacations. I told the woman we were in dire financial shape, that we had no intention of buying a timeshare, and that I would feel bad for the poor guy who had to have us for his presentation with no hope of making a sale. She insisted that the salesman would get paid either way, and it sounded like we needed a vacation.

"Tell your salesperson you're only doing it for the vacation," she said, "and he or she will make your presentation shorter." However, they only had one weekend available, December 17-19, which just happened to be our anniversary weekend.

The grandparents were all too happy to watch the girls for us. I asked the neighbors to watch our dogs and gave them a key to our house should they have an emergency.

When we returned, there was 200 dollars in cash on our kitchen counter. The two neighbors who knew we needed food took a collection among all the neighbors and their extended families. Now, we had money to buy Christmas gifts for the girls! I had written off Christmas, so now a secret desire of my heart was fulfilled for my girls.

That surgery I needed—I wanted to have it done before the end of the year because I had already met my insurance deductible, and the deductible would start over on January 1. The doctor had no appointments remaining for December. Then, out of the blue, she called to tell me she was coming home a day early from her vacation and she would do the surgery on Saturday, December 29, to make sure I could get it done at no further cost to me.

So, 2002 had begun with the threat of miscarriage, and continued with a high-risk pregnancy, followed by financial hardship, but it had ended with provision, protection, and even money to celebrate our anniversary and Christmas. God loves to work on my control freak nature. In my view, He intervened just in the nick of time. But from His perspective, He was on time, and He knew the plans He had for us. That year, I had constantly felt that God was failing me. Why would He allow two good, tithing Christians to get so low on food, baby supplies, and other basic needs? Why were we struggling week to week, paycheck to paycheck? What about that abundance and blessing I had always heard about? We not only were tithers, we gave to missions, special offerings, and the building fund. Why were we struggling?

I kept thinking, *God where are you?* In my obsessive-compulsive mind, God wasn't doing things right. He wasn't operating on my timetable. He knew I had a tendency to freak out. But He was on time, His time. He wanted to bring about His glory, to teach me to be more dependent on Him, and to show me He not only would provide for our needs, but He would give us some of our wants and desires, too. He also showed me the intensity of my pride and began to break down its first layer. I ended the year happily scrapbooking God's provision with photographs of the pantry, fridge, and the new coat we had purchased for Erica.

Dan had remained faithful and steady throughout the year. He said he just knew God would provide because His Word said He would. It reminded me of an old song that I had heard sung in a church play time and again, "God will make a way when there is no way, God will make a way for you!" Dan believed that, and I had thought I did. Dan's faith was firm and solid. He never wavered. I was grateful for all God had done, but I didn't understand the calm Dan possessed during that year. He had a peace that I didn't understand. He totally trusted God at His Word. I wanted that kind of faith and trust. Mine had grown, but my trust was still below average for someone who had been a Christian more than twenty years.

At the end of the year, my father-in-law's doctor cautioned that he had diabetes and needed to lose some weight. One day, after he already had dropped some pounds, my father-in-law happened to have an itch on his chest and felt a lump he had never felt before. Because his father had passed away from cancer, he took lumps very seriously. He went to see his doctor and learned that he already was between stage three and four breast cancer. We women are reminded constantly to do self-checks and have routine mammograms, but doctors don't encourage self-checks for male patients.

My father-in–law had been a marine. He didn't want this disease to dictate his life. His appearance would drastically change, and I was concerned with how Sydney would react to his hair falling out. I was beginning to see that Sydney did not react well to changes and transitions. George knew that hair loss would be an issue with chemotherapy and radiation, but he didn't want to lose his hair on cancer's terms. So, we decided to do a hair cutting party.

We told Sydney that George, who we called *Honey*, wanted to have short hair just like her daddy, who keeps his head shaved. We threw the party at Grammy and Honey's house, so Dan could shave his father's head. This was hard for my husband at first, knowing what it signified, but we adults kept up our smiling faces. We did a good job because Sydney was running around, singing and dancing about it, and Erica sat on the floor and clapped.

In summer 2003, I had a difficult choice to make about Sydney's education. She was turning five, and because her birthday month was October, I had to decide whether to start her in kindergarten, where she would most certainly be the youngest, or have her repeat transitional kindergarten as the oldest student. She already was showing signs of high intelligence, and I worried about holding her back. I wasn't sure if my gut feeling about her IQ was motherly bias or fact. Her preschool teachers had always commented that she was "gifted," often arguing for bumping her ahead to the next class.

Sydney had done traditional kindergarten at age three and four and had excelled in the schoolwork. Teachers validated that her vocabulary, overall knowledge, and reading capability were excellent for her age. In fact, her pediatrician really hoped I would put her in Montessori school. I decided to have her tested by a psychologist, and the test results did show above average intelligence. The consensus was that it was better for her to be the youngest in the class, so she could be challenged academically. After all, I started school young because of my October birthday, and I'd had no ill effects. In fact, I went on to skip a grade and graduate at sixteen. We figured that if Sydney were behind socially, she would have the opportunity to watch older students model proper behaviors. Despite everything that has happened to her in her education through the years, I maintain that this was the best decision for her, even considering the challenges we soon would have to overcome.

For most of Sydney's life, we had thought she was extremely bright. She had some quirks with her sensory processing and she struggled with transitions, but we saw nothing that would give us any real indication of the road ahead. She seemed to be developing normally, and she was an easy child, except for potty training and the eye patches.

When I began to write this book, I stopped right here for almost a year. I dreaded going back down the path of my daughter's elementary education. Those four to five years were filled with intense struggle and deep emotional and spiritual pain. Part of what made this so painful was the revelation of my own personal weaknesses and imperfections. I didn't want to even put into print the things I felt and struggled with during this phase of life. It was still too hard.

Even now, as I write this section, I continue to stop and cry as I process those years. I thought I had forgiven and moved past some of this, but each page reveals how much pain is still inside. I had considered leaving out any detail about my struggles, but as I have begun to speak and teach, my personal story is what seems to minister to people. So, with dread, I write this for all to see.

As this section gets underway, I am in Costa Rica on my first out-of-country mission trip. A woman with three decades of ministry experience is leading our mission team, and we are here to educate women about sexual and physical violence and how to heal from these experiences. The speaker has shared a painful experience with these ladies about her daughter's kidnapping and assault. She spoke with candor about her pain and how it affected her and her husband spiritually and in their work as pastors. She spoke about the importance of sharing your testimony: "If people can't see your brokenness, they can't appreciate the value of God's redemption in you."

She was trying to get the women in this culture to take off their spiritual masks and tell their stories. She encouraged them to walk out their testimony in public; that no matter what had happened in the past, their personal value to God has not changed. They are just as valuable as anyone else to the God who created them, despite the abuse they may have lived through. This validated for me that my personal story would be used somehow, in some way, for God's glory.

I know the power of personal testimony. I grew up in a church where, in the old days, on Sunday nights people would testify about what God had done in their lives that week. Two years prior to this mission trip, I had begun sharing small parts of my testimony, in workshops, seminars, sermons, small groups, and larger women's groups. I have written sermons based around Revelation 12:11, about "overcoming by the blood of the Lamb and the word of their testimony." But this is the first time I have laid it all out in one story.

When I was in college, I learned that as a counselor one should maintain a high degree of professionalism at all times. Studies show that when the client believes you are competent, in control, and professional, their confidence that counseling can be helpful increases. Your clients need to see you as the one who can help bring a solution to their issues, and the professional relationship is a huge key in this process.

For that reason, the counselor should never disclose personal matters or stories with clients. This provides emotional boundaries between the client and the counselor. It also keeps the focus on the client and does not burden them with the counselor's personal issues. The clients obviously have their own issues or they would not be in counseling.

When I was in the throes of Sydney's struggles, I was a licensed professional counselor, doing private practice, and teaching self-help classes to women, but I kept the façade that everything was going great in my personal life. I was professional in every setting. If you asked me how I was doing, I would say, "Fine." No one but close friends and family knew what I was dealing with on the inside. I asked pastors and friends in ministry for guidance and help, but this area of struggle was new in the church, and they couldn't really offer much assistance.

So, I kept my counselor mask on while I juggled life and circumstances. Most people thought I had an easy life, and that's what I wanted them to think. I was convinced, as many counselors and ministers are today, that if clients saw the true me—my challenges, my pain, my imperfections—they couldn't learn from me. If I showed my true self, people would think I had nothing to offer.

It was against this backdrop that Sydney's problems began to unfold and life turned upside down in the Holmes household. When I finally began to open up and share morsels of my story, one client said, "I'm so glad you are a real person and not super woman. When I thought you were perfect, I had a hard time coming to you."

When Sydney started kindergarten, I had a mixture of emotions. I felt sad that my baby was now going off to school all day, every day. Yet, I felt freedom that maybe now I could accomplish more during the day. I had two bright and beautiful girls, and I would now have more one-on-one time with the second one and could start to optimize her learning. I had a sense of joy that our first was reaching a huge milestone, that she was beginning formal education and gaining some independence. I had no reason to think anything would be out of the ordinary. Mothering had seemed so easy. I thought this next phase would be just as easy, because my professional training had armed me with the knowledge of childhood development and how to optimize education for children.

Because I hadn't yet gone back to full-time work, I was looking forward to the time alone with Erica. I was working six to eight hours a week at a home for young women with abusive pasts who were learning to overcome earlier mistakes and choices. If my mom or mom-in-law wasn't available to watch Erica, I brought her with me to the home, and the young women could have "baby therapy time" with her while I was in session. Erica also was a wonderful baby, and the young women loved it when I brought her for a visit.

Kindergarten started off great for Sydney. She had the same teacher that she adored from the previous year in transitional kindergarten; they even met in the same classroom. She excelled and didn't get into a single disciplinary situation. She breezed through her lessons and homework—until November. That's when she began to act out, as they say in school.

According to her teacher, she was misbehaving in class and becoming a disruption. She was excelling academically, even reading at second grade level, but her behavior had started to change noticeably. Her teacher was shocked at the conduct she was seeing. Sydney hadn't received one check on the board or one time-out the previous year. What was going on?

Sydney had come into her kindergarten year expecting it would be exactly same as the previous year in transitional kindergarten. TK had included both a full-week program and a Monday-Wednesday-Friday program. Sydney was the only student in the full-week program, so on Tuesdays and Thursdays, she'd had the teacher and the classroom to herself.

However, in kindergarten, she had to share the teacher and the classroom every day. Not only that, but the school had combined the TK and kindergarten classes into one room. The teacher had to teach two classes and expected more seatwork time from the kids not being taught. They were to sit quietly and do work while she taught the other class.

Can you imagine how this must have felt to a five-year-old? Later, through therapy, we learned what was going on in Sydney's mind: *Who are these kids? And why are they here every day now? Tuesday and Thursday are my days! The teacher seems to be frustrated with me more this year. Last year, she always said how good I was!*

Sydney started to become inconsolable if the teacher made any change to the schedule. If she changed the desks around in the classroom, Sydney acted as if her life were about to end. If someone touched or moved things on her desk, she would yell and maybe even run from the classroom. Sometimes, in a fit of rage, she would throw the items off of her desk. Maybe she would refuse to go to lunch or recess, or she might hide under a desk and refuse to come out.

Who was this child? The teacher couldn't be talking about my daughter? We had seen some anxiety if we moved things around at home, but we had never witnessed any of these behaviors. They seemed to be specific to school.

At home, she could be ornery or precocious, but we had never seen her lash out and throw things. Sometimes, she would say things over and over when she wanted something, so my husband and I called her "Rain Man," after the autistic man in the 1988 movie, but we certainly didn't think in any way she was autistic. We said it in jest when she was stressing out over something small.

We knew her memory skills were exceptional, and she liked a certain order to her room. It was unusually clean for a girl her age. We often called it a museum because she was always collecting things and putting them in some kind of order. At this stage, she collected rocks, paperclips, stuffed animals, and McDonald's toys, along with the bags they came in. None of that seemed odd or bizarre. Everything had its place.

Sometimes, just for fun while she was at school, I would make one small change to the order of something to see if she would notice. I might change two stuffed animals or dolls and see if she would notice. This was, of course, before her diagnosis. I saw it as a memory game. She would walk into her room and in mid-sentence stop and say, "Hey, how did Snow White get there? She doesn't live there." She would then put Snow White back in her place. She never suspected I moved them because the movie Toy Story was very popular then, and she assumed that, just like the movie, toys must move when they aren't being watched. She would get frustrated that the doll was out of place, but she never had a meltdown over it.

By Christmas, Sydney's behavior at school was escalating. If the teacher asked her to put something away, or if another student accidentally bumped her desk, she would go into anxiety mode. Depending on what the teacher did next, this might lead to rage, temper tantrums, and aggression. She was becoming more agitated at home, and she was very anxious about going to school. She used to love school, but now all I heard was how much she hated it. She was feeling this way because, as a result of her anxious responses in class, she was missing out on fun things, like art or recess, and instead had to clean up something she had thrown.

It began to dawn on me that Dan and I were making references to her acting like Rain Man more and more often. We were noticing more and more eccentric behaviors. Autism had crossed my mind, but she was so smart. I thought autism came with mental challenges, in addition to behavior issues. Sydney's acting out was mainly at school, so this didn't make sense to me. Early on, I had recognized her tendency toward perfectionism, but I chalked that up to DNA or maybe some budding OCD-type behaviors. Autism was only a fleeting thought that I dismissed it as soon as it came into my mind. In college I had learned that:

- Autism mostly occurred in boys.
- Autistic kids self-injure.
- Autistic kids get fascinated with spinning or focusing on a small part of something.
- Autistic kids have developmental delays.
- Autistic kids have problems with speech.
- Autism is really kind of rare. When I was in school it was one out of 5,000 kids.

For the most part, that is what was taught and mostly true at that time. I remembered a term I had heard in Developmental Psychology called *Asperger's Syndrome*. It was kind of like autism but thought to be really rare, and, again, mostly appeared in boys. Still, the word *Asperger's* would nag and nag at me. One day, I got out my Diagnostic and Statistical Manual out and looked it up. I saw a few things that seemed to fit, but then I dismissed it: Sydney is a girl, and she doesn't self-injure. She hates pain and avoids it, although she has a high tolerance for it.

I hung on to that one thing, telling myself Asperger's couldn't be the problem.

By January 2004, Sydney's adverse behaviors were so frequent, I was getting a call once a week to pick her up from school early. Other times, it was to come to the school to administer some form of discipline or to rescue the teacher from one of Sydney's throwing and yelling tirades. Soon, it became, "Just come get her."

By February, the calls were coming two to three times a week for me to come pick her up—immediately! By the end of the month, the school said they were going to put her on a three-strike policy. On the third strike, she would be permanently expelled and not allowed to return to school. *Well*, I thought, *my daughter was not going to be expelled from Christian school and certainly not in kindergarten. This called for drastic reinforcement measures.*

We had already been doing some positive reinforcement with stickers at home, but it was time to ramp it up. I looked up techniques from psychology books about token systems and charts and how to eliminate unwanted behaviors. This was nothing that good ol' cognitive–behavioral techniques couldn't whip into shape. Sydney was bright, so this would be easy.

My house was beginning to look like a group home or mental hospital ward. We had daily, weekly, and monthly charts placed around the house with clear-cut measurable goals and clearly delineated consequences and rewards. She had two phenomenal weeks. I thought I had found the answer and we were making permanent headway. Perhaps she was just a strong-willed child who needed her course corrected? Then, in one week, she got all three strikes, and we got the call to come get her. Her stuff was packed and ready to go, for there would be no need for our family to return to campus.

Sydney wasn't allowed to say goodbye to her friends. She wasn't allowed to meet up with her class at the field trip she had been anticipating so eagerly. She had been Jekyll and Hyde, and the school was done with these behaviors. Sydney got depressed; she had no understanding of why she couldn't return to school or see her friends. The school had called her behaviors sin and naughty, so she was having her first spiritual crisis at age five. Why didn't her teacher love her? Why didn't the Christians want her? What was wrong with her that made her act so crazy? Maybe God didn't like her, either. In later years, Sydney said she felt betrayed by the school, like they didn't understand her. This became the root of bitterness.

What was so befuddling to me, though, was that I knew this

child was overall a sweet person. Sydney looked out for people. She was very protective of those she loved and was always making a card or craft for someone. She loved animals, and she loved her family. It appeared that for no reason at all, this alter ego would suddenly appear. When that persona arrived, she would be unkind, anxious, mad, and she would yell some downright hurtful things. My mind went clinical to schizophrenia or bipolar disorder because these two illnesses had great prevalence in my family. The books said children don't tend to manifest these types of behaviors.

Because she was expelled from private school and hadn't met public school birthday requirements for kindergarten, she wasn't allowed into public school. I homeschooled her for the rest of the school year, from March through May. I was bound and determined to give this girl a graduation, so we borrowed a cap and gown and had our own celebration at home. I even pulled out my grad school robe to make the event official. Her grandparents came to our home to witness this milestone. She loved that we sprayed her down with silly string when the ceremony was over. Life felt a little more normal that day, but it was far from normal.

During that short homeschool experience, my eyes began opening to the bigger issue at hand. I needed to learn a lot more, but the greatest challenge became getting other people to listen and understand.

When your daughter gets expelled from kindergarten and you're a licensed counselor and teacher in church ministry, it's embarrassing when everyone knows. I was supposed to be an expert in parenting. Instead, I was mortified and felt like a failure. How could I ever help another family when my own daughter gets expelled for misconduct, class disruption, and disrespecting authority? How had I messed up so badly? Was God punishing me? My psychology textbooks and cognitive-behavioral techniques seemed to be failing me. Who could I talk to about all this? In whom could I confide my feelings? Where does a counselor turn when he or she needs help? Does what Sydney struggles with have a name?

As Sydney worked on school at home for the remainder of kindergarten, I was blown away at how intelligent she truly was. I knew she had an excellent memory, so I thought perhaps she had simply memorized a lot of facts, but she really had a good grasp of vocabulary usage and a quick acquisition of new concepts. Well, that must be it then! She was just too smart for that school. She wasn't being adequately challenged, so she was acting out. It was a small Christian school, not even five years old, itself. They were still getting the kinks out. They still had combined grades in each classroom. I continued to dismiss some of the red flags of autism spectrum disorder with my newfound theory. Her intelligence simply exceeded the overall class.

In kindergarten, Sydney was reading above her grade level and her testing showed her vocabulary usage was at third grade. Her math skills were at second grade. Now, remember, she was the youngest child in her class. She turned five in late October, so I reasoned that her intellectual ability was years ahead of her social skills. This would all work itself out as she matured. I still struggled with how much she adored structure and order. And it was obvious that she had strong sensory aversions. Her preferences were exponentially more than the common likes and dislikes of childhood. OK, she didn't really like change, new situations, or new people, but with her intellect, she would eventually figure this all out.

The ministry for young women I had worked with was having financial difficulty and could no longer sustain a counselor position, so over the summer I secured a part-time job at the school associated with my church. Erica would be able to attend the preschool, Sydney would be in first grade, and I could be right there to deal with any behavior mishaps. All three of us would be on the same campus. I thought with the right environment, being here at her home church, it would help Sydney feel safe and secure and help with some of her issues dealing with change.

Since my mom, my mother-in-law and I all worked at this location, she would be less likely to act out or try to "get me." I had asked Sydney's pediatrician if she thought Sydney had autistic tendencies. Her theory was that because Sydney was the youngest in her grade, she was socially immature. Her acting out at school was attention-seeking behavior. She felt like Sydney was jealous of the time I was spending with her younger sibling and was behaving this way to get time with me. That seemed like a plausible theory. She also said Sydney was too bright and high functioning to have autism and that perhaps at the small country school, she simply was not being academically challenged. With that reassurance, I shelved the autism label.

If Sydney were trying to gain my attention, I would be on campus to eat lunch with her, attend her chapel services, or even be a guest reader in her classroom. I could arrange my schedule to spend time with her during the school day. She would be in a larger, more established Christian school and get the academic challenge she needed while having the safety net of being at her home church with family around during the school day. I thought this was the solution.

The structure of the classrooms there was excellent, and the teaching staff was wonderful. Sydney was given a fabulous, sought-after teacher, and I just knew this was it. I was upfront with the headmaster, who was also a staff pastor at the church. I described Sydney's behavior issues at her previous school and told him she had some quirky behaviors. I admitted that I had some suspicions about autism, but I was determined that this would be a successful placement for her. The headmaster and teacher were onboard. They expressed determination to help Sydney have success in her new school environment.

The headmaster assured us that this first-grade year would be a new start, "She will be a new student starting out with a clean slate," he said. "Maybe she just needs that bull's-eye removed from her back as the bad behavior target. We will love her through this!" On more than one occasion, he said to Sydney and me: "We're in this for the long haul," or, "We love you; we are your church." He even said, "You aren't going anywhere, kiddo; you are welcome here!" This made Sydney feel very secure and more confident.

Sydney was showing some excitement again toward school. As I patted myself on the back, we were off and running for first grade. Now, during my three months of homeschooling, Sydney I had learned some pointers, and I passed those along to the teacher and headmaster:

- *If the desks are going to be moved or rearranged, if at all possible, warn Sydney. If you can, leave her desk in the same place.* She did not like her space and stuff moved. The teacher did an excellent job of this and let Sydney know when the décor or desks might change.

- *Never, ever, ever demand straight on, full eye contact if you are reprimanding Sydney. Never, ever get down on one knee to her level and put your hands on her head or shoulders. Never touch her while you are administering discipline. Do not hug her, unless she starts the hug position first. Touching her sets off the temper tantrums. Better for the adult to remain standing with a good distance between her and Sydney. Allow her to sit or crouch on the floor. She is listening, just not looking at you. Do not even touch her to comfort her when she is upset, unless she initiates or asks for a hug. Confining her, even with a hug, usually meets resistance and causes meltdowns.*

I had suggested two simple rules to navigate the behaviors and whims of Sydney Holmes. They go against everything educators are taught about instructing or dealing with a student. Most adults expect a child to look at them when being spoken to, and certainly if the child is being reprimanded or disciplined. Many are taught that a child feels safer and less intimidated if you get down on their level, versus lording over them as the tall adult. I didn't quite understand why the opposite worked for Sydney, but in disciplining her at home I had picked up on what escalated into a meltdown and what didn't.

I am a more authoritative or confrontational parent. I grew up in that kind of home environment. You'd better not talk back to an adult, run away, or make any disrespectful gesture with your body, face, or tone of voice. Period! When Sydney was younger and I was reprimanding her, she often would run and hide in her closet or under her bed. I mistakenly would follow after her, pull her out from under the bed or out of the closet, demand eye contact, and reprimand the disrespectful behavior. Because I had no idea that this was autism spectrum disorder (ASD), I saw her as a strong-willed child who needed strong boundaries.

This style of parenting is crushing to the ASD child. I finally learned that her hiding and getting in a small place was her way of trying to calm down. If I waited and let her get calm, my next interactions would go more smoothly. If I allowed her to sit on the floor, looking down while I talked to her, there was less anger and anxiety. If I kept my distance and did not touch her during the interaction, she would be able to better receive the correction and move on more quickly.

I didn't have a manual. This was just what seemed to work best. It was against everything I knew and totally against my confrontational personality. So, having explained all of this to those who needed to know, it appeared we were all on the same Sydney page. In Christian schools, you do not have an Individualized Education Plan (IEP) or an official 504. You have to shake hands on it and have faith. The teacher and I had an understanding about Sydney's seating preference, her "stuff," and the fact that she would be warned about any change in class structure or décor. The teacher was amazing and very understanding. All adults knew not to touch her or make any sudden moves toward her if she required correction. The headmaster kept reinforcing that she was, "here to stay." Sydney believed that, and so did I.

Chapter Six
Of Meltdowns and Closets

Before long, a slow downward spiral of behaviors began to rear its ugly head. I wish I'd had a book to read ahead and see what was going to happen, but I didn't. I had no idea of the depths of the issues and challenges my little girl possessed.

Sydney had her first major meltdown of first grade in the latter part of the fall. She had done quite well from August to early October. She had some close calls over incidents like having to erase things on her paper and not wanting to start over, or mishearing the order given on spelling tests and not wanting to change the words to the correct order, but she didn't have a major ordeal. She may have gotten stubborn and thrown her pencil or balled up the paper, but so far no hitting, screaming, or running away.

Why couldn't she roll with the punches like the other kids? What could cause a six-year-old child to get so distressed? Because she had no impulse control and she had difficulty communicating her feelings, all the adult saw was a meltdown for what seemed like no reason. This is no fault of the teacher or any other adult. It was mind-boggling. How did this sweet little girl turn into a fury of emotion so quickly? Many times, someone on the autism spectrum cannot tell you what it was exactly that upset them or triggered the anxiety or rage.

It took me weeks to get out of Sydney what was troubling her—the change in décor. The classroom had started out with "Welcome

Back to School" décor, and classroom rules posted on the walls. In late September or early October, it changed to a fall theme. These seemingly insignificant changes felt to Sydney as if she was in a brand-new classroom. The teacher had warned Sydney and did not move her desk, but that first week in the new décor was overwhelming to my daughter. If the new décor was not symmetrical, or the colors were too bright or too dull, it affected her ability to focus and self-regulate.

It took until Sydney was in third grade to put this pattern together completely. You could count on the first major meltdown of the school year happening in October. Another would come after the break from Thanksgiving, then another after the return from Christmas break. Expulsion would follow in March, after the biggest meltdown Sydney could display.

At Sydney's six-year checkup at the end of October, we began a trial of the drug Adderall. The thought was that maybe her lack of impulse control was related to ADHD. On 2.5 mg of Adderall, she was asleep by 10 a.m. each day. It knocked her out completely. The medicine certainly tamed the behavior, but it was an impediment to learning. Then, the rebound affect made her incredibly grumpy and difficult to be around when it came out of her system around 3 p.m. This medication didn't appear to be giving us the desired results. How a stimulant was putting her to sleep I never understood, but between sleeping an hour at school, having no appetite, being extremely grumpy and moody from 3 p.m. until dinner, and then not feeling sleepy at bedtime, it appeared the situation was worse and not better. We needed a new theory.

I began to research pediatric bipolar disorder because, as I've mentioned, bipolar is very common on one side of my family. But that was not a match. I wondered about her two major meltdown months being October and March and thought about seasonal affective disorder, but what about the other times she had meltdowns?

Neither of these solutions touched the fact that she did not like change. The fact that changes in her classroom triggered a meltdown was not really symptomatic of bipolar or seasonal affective disorder. What about the fact that she didn't like change in routine, or schedule, or in the order of things in her bedroom? We had bought her new, big-girl bunk beds and furniture that year. I was irate when after only a few weeks, she had taken a pen and written the different types of underclothes and pajamas she had and was tick marking on the dresser how many times she wore each, so she could make sure she was wearing them an equal numbers of times. Seriously? She showed me her marking system so proudly, and I about had a meltdown myself! Permanent marker on the new furniture? My reaction was not what she had hoped. In fact, I crushed her little heart when I freaked out. Mr. Clean Magic Erasers saved her life that day, probably. They've become a huge asset to my family. I just keep them on hand.

When Sydney had her meltdown in October, I had to pick her up from school early, and she was not allowed to return until the following day. There was no talk about chances, check marks, or how many more times. We were reassured that this had to happen to teach her boundaries, but "she was here to stay." She had some minor instances of disruption from October through Christmas break, but there was no major hitting, kicking, or spitting.

Sydney's problems were focused more around having to re do something because of her perfectionist tendencies. Sydney hated to erase and re write. She hated how the paper looked and felt after erasing. This made me suspect obsessive-compulsive disorder (OCD). If you didn't know Sydney and you observed her complaining about re doing something, you would certainly think she was disrespectful or obstinate. Her teacher never called her *disrespectful*. She said she enjoyed having Sydney in her class. Sydney could be trying at times, but the teacher was getting pretty good at redirecting her. We all thought things were moving along quite successfully.

The new calendar year got off to an OK start in January. Sydney had seventy-two straight days of no behavior outbursts. I still have the behavior chart we kept as proof. Seventy-two straight days! I was amazed. She was learning how to navigate these situations a little better. Her teacher's patience, kindness, and helpful attitude certainly helped encourage Sydney to stay in control. I wish all of her elementary teachers could have had the insight this teacher did, and this teacher was not trained in special education! My daughter understood that this teacher cared about her. This helped her to try harder to comply, as she didn't want to disappoint the teacher.

I thought maybe we had turned that major hurdle. From

Christmas to March, I thought maybe I was dealing only with OCD and a strong-willed child. I was letting ASD go because, after all, seventy-two days was quite the feat. Then came that fateful Wednesday in March. My chest had been hurting, and I had heard that someone at work had been diagnosed with pneumonia. I decided to go to the urgent care that was less than a mile from the school, so I could be back in time to get Sydney at the end of the school day. They did chest x-rays, and it took far longer than anticipated to get the results. I did have double pneumonia. No wonder I felt so lousy. I was going to be about five or ten minutes late getting Sydney, but the teacher already knew that if I were late they could call my mom or mother-in-law to get her. They knew not to put her in after-school care.

In fact, that very morning Sydney was freaking out about the thought of having to go to after-school. She hated after-school. It was too noisy. I had reminded her it was Wednesday and, because of church, we never did after-school on Wednesday. After several reassurances that she would not go to after-school, she went happily to class. But on this day, the teacher assistant was handling the after-school dismissal. I was fifteen minutes late. The rule at the school was if a parent was fifteen minutes late, the child was sent to after-school. Why the assistant didn't remember that my mom and mother-in-law were on location, I will never know. My mom signed the paychecks; she was not hard to remember. The regular teacher knew never to send Sydney to after-school on Wednesdays. But the assistant put Sydney in the after-school line, and the meltdown ensued.

First came anxiety; Sydney repeated over and over that it was Wednesday, and she did not do after-school on Wednesdays. When the teacher assistant would not listen and kept quoting the school rule, Sydney began to throw her books and book sack and run. She refused to get in the after-school line. At this point, I had entered the building but was stopped by a parent asking me a question about their student's grades. I had no idea all hell had broken loose on the bottom floor. I thought that they would have had my mom pick up Sydney. That had been protocol all year. Instead, the assistant panicked because she felt the other children were in harm's way, and she paged the headmaster.

The headmaster came down, and the meltdown was in full

swing. Instead of following the protocol I had set up, he decided to do it his way. He got down on one knee, placed his hands on her shoulders, and told her it was time to calm down and get in line as she was told. She told him to go away, and he kept the hold on her shoulders, trying to control her. She spit in his face, which made him remove his hands and back up. He remained on her level, trying to reprimand her while she was coming unglued. He told her that spitting was not OK, and he demanded eye contact. She refused. He demanded an apology. She refused. He got close to her again to put his hands on her shoulders, and she hit him in the face and told him to go away.

Without one word to me, without discussing this or offering so much as a goodbye, he instructed the teachers to pack up all of Sydney's stuff. She was not to return to the classroom. She was gone.

I arrived right after this and found an out-of-sorts child sitting with her stuff packed in brown paper bags. The teacher assistant was still in shock, and the teacher had returned during the end of the meltdown. She had tried to plead Sydney's case. She said Sydney was doing so well. This was unusual.

The headmaster was embarrassed, essentially. He felt as if he was losing his authority in the eyes of the teachers who saw the tantrum and the students who were waiting to go to after-school. He wasn't even there to tell me. He had the teacher tell me that Sydney was permanently suspended. End of discussion. Period. No turning back!

I had just been diagnosed with double pneumonia and was already feeling lousy, but now I was irate. I was irate with Sydney for acting that way. I was upset that the assistant didn't remember to call my mom. I was furious with the headmaster, who also was my boss, for not following the two simple instructions on how to deal with my daughter.

This was a hard blow. The school was part of the ministry of the church we belonged to. My family had attended for more than twenty years, as one of four remaining founding families. My mom had worked at the church and school for more than ten years. I was employed by the school.

The headmaster was not only my boss but also an associate pastor. I would still see him six days a week. Every Sunday, Sydney would be reminded of her expulsion. She hated him. She called him a liar and the church a liar! She never wanted to go back. The situation was painful for me on so many levels. I felt betrayed.

Now, I would have no choice but to put Sydney in public school. No other Christian school would take a twice-expelled kid. I lived forty-five minutes away from the church—which meant my daughter would be in school in the town where we lived, and I would have to go in to work, then cut the day short to get back to pick her up from school. This was a huge imposition. I was angry and hurt, and I would be reminded every work day that my boss and associate pastor broke his word and expelled my daughter. Every Sunday my daughter would walk past her old classroom and ask, "Why can't I go back to school? He said I was here forever. I hate him. He lied."

It took Sydney nearly three years to work through this. She told me later, in fourth grade, that she missed that first grade teacher. She never got to say goodbye. She would tear up and cry. Then, she admitted that she held on to that anger for all that time.

"That's when I decided I must be bad," she said. "My own church did not love me. If that pastor didn't want me and he lied to me, I must be really, really bad, and I shouldn't try hard anymore." That day was such betrayal to her. Why did the seventy-two days of good behavior not count for something?

She said she felt that if her own church and school couldn't love her, how could God love her? She actually wished she had never been born. She recounted the headmaster's words of never giving up on her.

She said, "If the pastor and headmaster would lie to me and not love me, how can I trust anyone? How can I believe anyone loves me or wants me?" I tried to explain the behavior she exhibited that day, but her black and white thinking was stuck on, "The church lied." From this expulsion in first grade, her behavior and will to maintain any form of self-control eroded. She was a child without hope.

We moved her to a public school, and the rest of first grade was a disaster. When we arrived at the new school, I pulled the teacher aside to confide in her that, although Sydney did not have a diagnosis, I strongly suspected autism as the final clue to why she was struggling with behavioral breakdowns at school. I asked her to consider that fact when disciplining Sydney and to show kindness and mercy to her because she was still in shock from having to change schools and was very sad about this transition. I tried to convey that I wanted us all to be on the same page regarding the fact that Sydney was not a behavior problem, but we simply did not know what was causing this conduct.

March through May was worse than a nightmare. This was a larger school, with more students in the class and, therefore, more noise. Sydney was in trouble for something nearly every day. She did not care. Within the first two weeks, she had her first major incident, resulting in my having to leave work to get her. This episode was triggered when she didn't understand the teacher's instructions. The teacher was older and had been teaching for twenty-five years. Everything that was not immediate obedience was considered willful disrespect and disobedience. The teacher knew that Sydney had been expelled from her previous school, so she was going to teach her a lesson.

The teacher had instructed the children to get their reading mats, pick a book, and read silently to themselves. Now, if there was anything Sydney loved about school at this point, it was reading time. She got the mat and book and began to read quietly. She was reading in a whisper, which is what she thought reading quietly meant. The teacher told her to stop being disobedient. Sydney had no idea what she was doing wrong, so she continued reading. The teacher counted to three and told her to stop or go to time-out.

Confused and now annoyed, Sydney told the teacher she was reading quietly. The teacher took that as disrespect and sent her to time-out. Sydney refused because she didn't know what she had done wrong. The teacher began to pick her up to put her in time-out, and the meltdown of the decade ensued. Sydney screamed, she emptied the bookshelves, threw the books, and went wild. The teacher called the principal and special education teacher to her room.

Now, I had told the new principal: "If Sydney ever is in a rage, never take her to your office. She will destroy it." Well, as I had seen others do in the past, he didn't listen. He took her to his office to calm her down, and she emptied his desk and shelves of anything she could get her hands on, all the while screaming at the top of her lungs.

Then, two female teachers took her shoes off, grabbed her by her hands and feet and took her to what Sydney called "the time-out closet," located in the special education classroom. She was struggling to get free, spitting, and screaming how she hated them and wanted them to die.

When she was put in the time-out room, they called me to come get her. All they said was that she had a meltdown, couldn't be consoled, and needed to go home. I was in the middle of teaching a class and had a forty-five-minute drive to get her. As I arrived inside, I heard a child screaming bloody murder. I recognized that scream, and with Erica on my hip, I took off running. Sydney was two halls over, and I could hear her screaming.

The teacher looked at me and said, "She's been disrupting the whole learning day for the entire student body for the last hour." She was snide and hateful. I arrived to the time-out closet, and it took everything in me not to slug these people for locking my daughter in this closet. Let me describe it: This was a closet—not a room—barely three-by-three feet. It had a concrete floor and no padding or carpet. The walls were unpadded, and the studs were exposed. The light bulb wasn't very bright, maybe twenty-five watts, so it was dark. Oh, and the best part was the door. It was a piece of thin plywood on hinges, and then it latched to keep her in. There was no window for her to see out or for them to look in to make sure she was not banging her head on the concrete floor.

After I got over the shock of what I saw and the urge to punch these teachers in the face, I put Erica down abruptly and unlatched the door to the closet. Sydney's knuckles were scraped from beating on the door to get out. Her toenails were broken off from kicking the door. Her face was swollen from the screaming and crying, and her voice was nearly gone. When I opened the door, she raised her fist as if to hit the intruder entering. She opened her eyes, saw that it was me, and collapsed into a heap on the floor of the closet.

My heart broke. The pain of this moment still brings tears to my eyes. This is what the great public school system thought was the best way to deal with my first-grader's issue? I walked inside the closet and shut the door behind me. Sydney climbed into my lap, shaking and saying she didn't do anything. She just kept saying, "I didn't do anything. I didn't do anything."

Think about this from her perspective. She has no idea she is doing anything wrong. She is grabbed up and taken to the office, then grabbed and placed into a dark closet. She was terrified. We sat there a few moments together until I could get her to calm down enough to walk on her own. She was whimpering and trying to catch her breath. I regained some composure, and we walked out together.

The principal and special education teacher were looking at me with sheer disgust.

The special education teacher said, "See, that was all for show. See how she stopped screaming when she saw you?"

The other teacher, said, "She doesn't have any form of autism. Autistic kids like small places; it calms them down. I read that autistic kids like small places."

I tried to have an intelligent conversation with the lead teacher. I reminded her that Sydney was undiagnosed, but I was fairly certain she had a higher functioning form of autism called, "Asperger's Syndrome."

The teacher crudely replied, "I've seen Rain Main, Mrs. Holmes. She does not have autism. Besides, autism is a boy's issue. She cannot have autism." Wow, how astute. She had seen a movie in the 1980s and diagnosed my daughter that quickly. She said in front of the principal and me that she purposely did not go into special education for a reason. She said that she didn't want that kind of child in her classroom. She did not want to teach Sydney.

I tried to be nice. I tried to remain calm.

"No child, whether autistic or not, would want to be manhandled, then thrown into a dark closet where they cannot see out," I retorted. I then turned to the other teacher and said, "Maybe she stopped crying when she saw me because I let her out! Did you think about that?"

Then, I turned to the principal, "Why did you take her to your office?"

All three just stood there like deer caught in the headlights. Sydney had calmed down. I asked her what happened. She said she didn't know. I asked the teacher, and she recounted the scene.

I got a book for Sydney and said, "Sydney, read silently." She began to whisper.

The teacher said, "See, she is disobeying. She is speaking!" Sydney started to get anxious again.

I sat down beside her with the book and said, "Read this right here, and don't move your lips, OK?" She said okay and complied. I then asked what she read. She told me. I said, "See, you read it without moving your mouth."

She looked accusingly at the teacher and said, "Why didn't you tell me that?" Reading silently was reading in your mind, not with your mouth? Sydney had no idea.

The other kids had been in that first-grade, public school classroom since August. Sydney had only been there a couple of weeks. She didn't understand the instructions and was accused of disobedience. I tried to explain to the three that if an ASD child is accused of something they believe they did not do, this is the way they would react. This was not disobedience; it was a misunderstanding that escalated. Grabbing her made it worse. Locking her in the room terrified her.

Well, they decided she needed to take a few days off from school. Sydney now had great anxiety about going to school at all. She was terrified of that closet. On top of that, she had to go to work with me, which meant going back to the Christian school building she had been expelled from before being forced to come to this school.

Her suspension extended into spring break, and I asked the principal to move her to another class when school resumed. The teacher didn't want Sydney, and there was no reason to set her up for failure.

During the break, we found a Christian counselor to help Sydney work on her anger, anxiety, and frustration. I was concerned that she was becoming depressed. Her counselor contacted the school about this closet Sydney had described in therapy. She thought for sure Sydney and I were exaggerating about its size. She made notes. She reported to me that if this room existed at the school, it was in violation of the North Carolina code for a time-out room. The fact that the door didn't have a window, the walls were unfinished, and the floor had no padding made this room illegal to use for discipline. I called the Department of Education and reported the room, and I was told later that the school was instructed to dismantle the room and to never use it again. Apparently, the people at the school district level had been unaware of the room's existence. The school became really mad at me.

Over spring break, we had to start preparing Sydney for a new teacher and a different classroom. She was less than enthusiastic about it, of course. She had transferred to this school in March and already had a teacher who didn't like her, she was locked in a time-out "closet," and now another change. In that first week after spring break, she had another major meltdown. The school decided a counselor should talk to her and scare some sense into her. I was asked to attend this session. The counselor told my six-year-old daughter that if she behaved like that again, they would call the police and she would end up in "juvey." Of course, Sydney didn't understand what that was, and the counselor was all too eager to explain that it was a terrible place with bad, scary, older kids, and she would not see her mommy or daddy. I was appalled at this tactic.

Since March, I had been begging and pleading and exhorting that Sydney be tested and evaluated, as by now I was certain she had some level of autism. The school essentially said it was too close to the end of the year and was not worth their time or energy. They said I should try the TEACCH Autism Program, which is known for its expertise. If TEACCH thought Sydney had ASD then the school would listen, but, at this point, they were still under the impression that Sydney was just a spoiled brat with an opinionated mom, and she needed more discipline. I called TEACCH that very day, but after they mailed me an information packet and I returned it to them, they said there was a nine-month waiting period. I felt helpless. That would mean another whole school year without a label or diagnosis.

What could I do to get Sydney help through these last six or seven weeks of first grade? There was no place to send her, and if I wanted to establish an IEP, I had to keep her in public school. It was so frustrating. When I called TEACCH back for some advice and told them what we'd been through, they sent someone to observe Sydney in the classroom and to begin making their evaluation.

This wonderful person spent three hours watching Sydney interact with others and pointing out to the teacher what behaviors seemed to fit Asperger's. It was not a formal diagnosis, but after the observation, the woman felt strongly that Sydney did indeed have ASD.

TEACCH tried to educate the lead teacher, the special education teacher, and staff, but these people had made up their minds. Sydney was a bad apple and, as far as all of them were concerned, this school year could not end fast enough! She got suspended a few more times, usually during PE and then on field day. I felt like those six weeks dragged on forever!

Sydney's anxiety was not the normal, garden-variety anxiety I'd learned about in graduate school. It was not just a generalized anxiety. Her rituals and compulsions were not just obsessive-compulsive behaviors. It was not just a social anxiety about new people and new places; it was all of this and more—on steroids!

How could a young child have so much anxiety? I knew we had to get her specialized help, but I didn't know where to go to find it. What I did know for sure was that she would not return to this school in the fall. It didn't matter that this was her district; somehow, some way, she would be anywhere but this place.

The final straw came when the school suggested holding Sydney back. Because she was the youngest in the class, they felt that social immaturity was causing her issues. Holding her back would help her socially and, thus, behaviorally. She had straight A-pluses in all subjects. She was already complaining that she was bored in class. Repeat the grade? That wasn't happening! These "experts" at the school were clueless, and I felt a sudden need to educate myself on all things Asperger's and to do so quickly! I had counted on the almighty public school with its special education staff and IEPs to help me, but they knew less than I did. Yet, they were supposed to be the ones making the decisions about my child's education.

Chapter Seven
Diagnosis Day

That summer we were pretty heavily involved in various forms of testing. I needed to go back to the school system for Sydney's second-grade year with something, some kind of label that said, "My child is not bad! She really does have a neurological issue. Please help her!" I had finished my paperwork with TEACCH and was on the nine-month wait list for the evaluation. That seemed to satisfy the school psychologist. In fact, she invited me to bring in Sydney during the summer for some intelligence-type testing. It was quite the ordeal. Over a period of a few days, the counselor administered the Woodcock-Johnson battery, the Peabody Picture Vocabulary Test, and the Wechsler Intelligence Scales for Children (WISC). During the Woodcock-Johnson testing, she stopped in the middle of the process to call me.

"I thought you signed the form saying your daughter had not been administered the Woodcock-Johnson in the last year."

"That is right. She hasn't."

"Then explain to me why she keeps saying, 'Last time I took this test I said this; but that is not right. It's this,' or, 'I remember that picture.'"

I said, "Well, she did take it when she was three or four years old, as an admittance test for T-K. That was nearly three years ago. Doesn't it strike you as odd that she would remember those exact questions for nearly three years?"

I was trying to prove my point that Sydney had Asperger's, but the counselor thought I must be coaching her on the test or something.

When the counselor scored the WISC, Sydney's overall IQ was 149. That is not just above average; it is way above average. When all of her tests came back at genius levels, the school psychologists concluded: "There is nothing the school can do. She has no academic problems; her problem is 100 percent behavioral."

Argh! Now, I am only a Master's degree level of counseling, but even in my testing classes, we were told to look at the discrepancies in the high and low scores. A ten- to fifteen-point discrepancy between language and math scores indicated there was some sort of learning issue. Sydney's lowest score in Reading Comprehension was 120. Her math score was 150. That is a discrepancy of 30 points. Follow the logic with me here. If ten to fifteen points suggest a learning discrepancy between the two halves of the brain, what did thirty points mean? I tried to explain that, although Sydney's overall IQ was 149, if her hardest subject, reading comprehension, was only 120, this meant reading was a struggle to her.

She is above average when compared to other kids her age, but when measured against her own abilities, there is a huge discrepancy between her math and language skills. But, according to the counselor, because Sydney was so smart, this point of discrepancy didn't apply. What?

Sydney loved to sit and read, and she had a huge vocabulary, but as with most kids on the spectrum, she didn't always understand what she read. She had no clue about the point of the story or what the author was trying to convey, and she especially did not understand dialogue between characters. If the passage used jokes or sarcasm, she completely missed it, and she couldn't follow tone.

As I would later learn, ASD kids do not understand the semantics of language. This is not an academic problem per se, but it does impact the ability to learn. I tried to explain how frustrating it is for someone who is so smart to not understand what they read, how this could hamper a student understanding instructions on a test, especially a standardized test. My pleas fell on deaf ears. The school was even more convinced—Sydney was smart. She did not have academic struggles. She had bad behavior that needed to be disciplined. They would not grant an IEP meeting. Case closed.

I called TEACCH and told them about the extensive testing. I told them we had seen a neurologist, psychiatrist, geneticist, and school psychologist. I was desperate. Sydney could not enter the new school year without a diagnosis, and we could not wait nine months on TEACCH. The woman had an idea. If I took Sydney off the wait list and put her on the will-call list, she could get moved up if someone else canceled. The catch was that if someone cancelled, I would have to drop whatever I was doing and go, even if it was during family vacation. I decided this was top priority and everything else could wait.

In the meantime, TEACCH said I could play the rule out game. All of the professionals we were seeing were trying to rule things out, but each professional focused on one piece of the puzzle. The counselor, who was also an R.N., had zeroed in on Sydney's anxiety and some of her depressed mood or flat affect. She noted that Sydney's anxiety got extremely high around change and new things and that this anxiety usually resulted in a meltdown. The counselor did see autistic characteristics in Sydney, but she wasn't certain if that was the issue.

She referred me to the pediatric psychiatrist. He was from India, and he felt that Asperger's was a made-up American disorder. He said they didn't have much Asperger's in India. It was a self-control issue, and we Americans do not discipline our children, and we want to label them, instead. After his evaluation, he suggested OCD and intermittent explosive disorder and maybe some oppositional defiant to boot. Both he and the counselor felt that Sydney had adjustment disorder. He suggested we try some medication to help with the aggression outbursts and the anxiety and mood issues.

All of the professionals noted Sydney's anxiety, her need for routine and structure, her difficulty adjusting to change, her meltdowns characterized by anger and aggression, and that she had high intelligence but no developmental delays. They saw a number of other concerns: noncompliance, sensory issues, her ability to place extreme focus on things she enjoyed, her lack of focus on things she did not enjoy, and her difficulty making friends with peers.

Two years earlier, an occupational therapist had diagnosed sensory processing disorder. Another fact I would learn is that nearly all ASD children have sensory issues. A red flag I did not know about, and, hence, had missed. So, if you look at the bigger picture, wouldn't Asperger's be a better diagnosis than OCD, ODD, sensory processing, IED, and adjustment disorder? Would it not make sense to give her a single diagnosis of Asperger's, which covered all of those symptoms, than to give her multiple diagnoses?

The pediatric psychologist wanted to further rule out neurological and genetic factors, so he sent us to the geneticist and the neurologist. The geneticist had to take vials and vials of blood. I cannot exaggerate how horrible that day was, holding Sydney down for the blood to be drawn. It did not go unnoticed by the geneticist. He did a full work-up and found no chromosomal abnormalities.

The neurologist wanted to make sure she wasn't having seizures or other glitches. She saw Sydney's reaction to the testing and did a symptom checklist for Asperger's. She said all indicators pointed to Asperger's, but she didn't feel confident in her assessment.

I was getting more and more desperate. If the experts did not know what to call it, what was I, the parent, supposed to do to help her? About that time, we got the phone call from TEACCH, the miracle call that the wait was over. A spot had opened up over the summer.

The TEACCH evaluation process was a six-hour ordeal. They had already seen her in the classroom setting for three hours, and they already suspected an Asperger's diagnosis but wanted to run the full evaluation. They observed her interacting with the evaluators. They observed her playing, her motor skills. I filled out tons of paperwork about my pregnancy, her development, her daily skills, her questionable behaviors, and I brought with me all the testing and evaluations from the other professionals. They sent us to a late lunch, and a team of four took two hours to compile the data and observations. The team consisted of a social worker, a counselor, a developmental psychologist, and an educational psychologist. I took Sydney to lunch and a local toy store for a prize after the long day of testing and interacting. I had a queasy feeling in my stomach. I knew what was coming, but it was about to be made official.

We returned to the center for the "What does this all mean?" talk. The team's diagnosis was Asperger's with mild OCD tendencies. They explained that no two children with autism present the same, that the old adage, "If you have seen one child with autism, you have seen one child with autism," is true. They added that this diagnosis is usually co-morbid with OCD, ADHD, or ODD and that her anxiety seemed to be more than just ASD. Even for an Aspie, she was excessively anxious about making mistakes, and her need for perfection was over the top.

They took a long time to explain what this meant for her future, what I needed to do at school, and then gave me two handwritten pages of suggestions for home and school settings. They said the IEP this upcoming year, second grade, would be crucial and that the Autism Society of North Carolina would be a great asset in that process. In fact, TEACCH and the Autism Society of N.C. were there for me, to educate me on what to do and how to do it, and what strategies to try. TEACCH said I should force the issue that Asperger's falls on the autism spectrum, and the school is legally bound to help Sydney. They even contacted the school system we were in and pressed for an IEP meeting ASAP to help her start at the new school with a valid plan.

Well, as I stated before, Sydney was not returning to the school that had locked her in the time-out closet. I went to the county's special education department and requested a transfer based on that school's inability to meet her autism needs. I wanted a district school closer to where I worked, in case I was called to come get her, and a school that had some understanding about Asperger's syndrome. A new school had just been built in our county only ten to twelve minutes from where I worked. The special education person said this principal knew Asperger's and would work with me to get an IEP that would help meet Sydney's autism and sensory needs in the classroom. Phew, what a relief! A principal that gets it; this was perfect!

I contacted the Autism Society, and they gave me pointers about what to ask for in the IEP and classroom setting. I thought I was armed and ready. I had read a lot about the use of shadows with high-functioning kids, someone who would follow the student from class to class and assist them as needed. I really wanted Sydney to have a shadow. I felt she could do the mainstream work, but she needed a helper for those tough trigger times.

I presented a strong case for a shadow and all the things the Autism Society told me to fight for, but I went in alone. It was me against the school. It felt like a car sale. You know, the salesman's job is to give you as little as possible for the higher price, and you want as much as you can for a lower price, so you try to meet in the middle. I thought the school would want to do whatever was necessary to help my child succeed. I mean, we are supposed to be operating under the principle of "No child left behind." My child should not be left behind! But I found out that as far as the law is concerned, students are only entitled to a free, appropriate, public education (FAPE, as it is referred to by law), and appropriate is defined by the powers that be. They do not strive to optimize the student's potential; they only provide the basic tools that the student with a disability would need to "succeed." I assure you, the school's definition of success and my definition did not match up.

That first IEP was really just to throw me a bone and keep me quiet, to say they did something. The plan was pretty bare; it included provisions for preferential seating, extra time on tests and quizzes, removal from stressful situations, and a goal to reduce anxiety with the use of the occupational therapy room. It was a start. Another positive for the school was that it was a peanut-free school, and Syd had a deadly peanut allergy.

OK, I conceded and figured something was better than nothing. I felt a little better that she would spend second grade in a peanut-free school, with a principal that understood Asperger's, and at least some of the items we requested were in the IEP. I did not get the shadow. The school district's attitude was, "We'll consider a shadow once these provisions fail." What I never understood was the concept of allowing a child to hit rock bottom before intervening. I am a fan of early prevention and maintaining the child's self-confidence.

When I got the school's handbook and began to look over some of the policies and the supply list, I could see signs that perhaps this principal didn't really understand Asperger's, especially the sensory issues.

This school was quite socialistic in terms of student supplies. The supply list was very specific about what was to be bought for the students' use. Everything had to be the same brand and color because all supplies were placed in a community pool in which no single student owned anything. It was all common use.

I understand trying to even the playing field for the haves and have-nots, but if an item is going to trigger a student's autism and sensory processing, it seems like that could be dealt with in the IEP. The two items that caused problems for Sydney were the scissors (metal, with no rubber grips) and the pencil grips chosen for the pencils. Both felt funny in her hand. They aggravated her, and using them triggered meltdowns. I appealed to the teacher and special education teacher: Because these were, in fact, sensory issues associated with the diagnosis of autism, could I get supplies that felt good to her and that she could keep in her desk?

The whole aspect of community sharing was not going over well. Sydney did not want to use a pencil grip everyone else had used; she wanted the ones we bought, the one that felt soft to her hand. This seemed like a battle the school could concede under the IEP. This was a need, not the selfish desire of a second-grader.

Another issue at this school which claimed to understand autism, was the seating arrangement. There is a misnomer that preferential seating should always be the front desk at the very top of the room. I cannot overstate this: The school should not have one standard rule for preferential seating. Preferential seating for someone with ADHD may be different than for someone with wheelchair access issues or who is blind or deaf or has autism. When you look at the autism spectrum, you have to know the child in order to know what seat will work for him or her. Maybe they need to be away from noise and distraction. Maybe they need to be beside a window or away from a window. Maybe they need to be front and center, but they may also need space from other students. Talking to the parent is crucial.

This teacher had arranged the desks in such a way that the students faced each other, so Sydney's desk touched the front of another student's desk and that made them have straight-on eye contact. When the teacher taught, students would turn their chair around to see the board, but when working at their desks they were facing the student in front of them. When we went in for orientation, I was very clear that this seating arrangement would not work. The teacher chose the desk in the front as the preferential seating for Sydney—the desk closest to the door—and seated her directly across from another student.

This teacher had no insight into ASD issues. I politely and gently pointed out to her that if the school insisted that Sydney use the supplies they wanted instead of ones that felt good on her hands, she was very likely to get frustrated with the metal scissors and fling them off her hand. That could be a problem with another student directly in front of her. Her intention wouldn't be to hit the student, but in a moment of frustration she wouldn't be processing the safety of others.

I pointed out that previous schools had said that Sydney was a runner. She could possibly dart out of the classroom and disappear. Being that close to the door was not the best seat choice. In fact, having her face any student with direct eye contact was not a good choice. Because there was an odd number of desks, I suggested the last desk on the front row, away from the door, because it was a single desk not facing any other student. This would give her front row access to the board, while also keeping her free from distractions. It would give the teacher a better chance of catching her if she decided to run out of the room, and if she flung scissors or threw her pencil, no one would get hurt. The teacher consulted with the special education teacher, and they decided the desk the teacher chose was in fact the preferential seat.

The special education teacher felt that perhaps I wasn't giving Sydney the benefit of the doubt, that she was one grade older and more mature and might not run out of the room. They explained all the things the other school did wrong and said that because they were starting with an IEP, Sydney wouldn't have any problems.

OK, I had given my warning, based on earlier expulsions (prior to TK, in kindergarten, and in first grade) already, regarding what worked and what didn't. I warned that they were putting the student in front of Sydney in harm's way when (not if) she got frustrated with those stiff scissors.

While I was there, I also brought up the issue of Spanish. There are certain sounds in the Spanish language that are irritating to Sydney, and the Spanish class was usually a trigger for her running out of the classroom. If she didn't run, she would just sit there covering her ears. The teachers told me I was worrying for nothing. I would see, Sydney would just love this new school so much; she would want to do anything to make it work.

So, I tried to educate them. We spent the rest of the orientation day walking up and down the halls of the school. Sydney wanted a map, so she could memorize where everything was located: bathrooms on every hall, main office, stairs, access to outside, and emergency exits. Because spectrum kids are also behind on gross motor skills, outdoor activities on playground equipment can be problematic. Over the summer we had come to the school on the weekends and practiced using the equipment, so Sydney would not be anxious and feel humiliated that she couldn't handle the monkey bars or other climbing equipment. That orientation day we went out and practiced one more time, and she had some confidence that she could do it. So, I will just focus on that positive for one second.

Usually, it takes a school the first few weeks to coordinate special classes, like Spanish, with the regular schedule. When the schedule was finalized and Spanish became a two-day-a-week class, trouble started. It became the weekly problem. I could guarantee I would get a call from the school during Spanish class. The pattern went like this: The teacher would come and begin speaking English, but with her strong accent Sydney would cover her ears. She would be told to uncover them, and she would refuse. She would be called upon to say a word in Spanish and would refuse, with an outright "No!" When the Spanish teacher threatened to put her in time-out or send her to the principal's office, this would trigger a meltdown that would disrupt the class. She might even run out of the room. One day, she got so frustrated about being told to go the principal's office, she turned her desk over and began to throw whatever she could find at the teacher, screaming "No!" Then, when they called for backup, she bolted out of the room.

Sydney got suspended for this incident in order to teach her a lesson, they said. After six weeks of me suggesting that she not take Spanish, they added to her IEP that she was excused from this special class. But for six weeks she had been melting down twice a week, and these incidents would set the tone for the rest of the day. She dreaded Spanish so much that on those days just getting her into the car to go to school became a problem. Years later, I learned that the sound of the Spanish words actually hurt her ears. This is part of the sensory stuff the school just didn't comprehend, not even the special education director.

The moment that I had feared finally came, the moment I had specifically warned the teacher about on orientation day.

Upon interviewing those who saw the incident, I learned the following: It was time to practice cutting skills—with, you guessed it, the bulky, metal, stiff scissors. Sydney did not want to use them. She complained that they hurt her hand, and she was refused. The teacher told her she had to finish the task or take it home for homework. She hated homework. She began to cut with the scissors but got tired of them and did not want them touching her any longer. She held up her hand and flung them off.

Remember that other student they placed directly in front of her? Yep, that was not a good idea. As the scissors flew through the air they grazed the boy's head and scared him, so he yelled out. He was not hurt at all, thankfully, but he was startled by the scissors and by Sydney's yelling.

The teacher freaked out. She lectured Sydney about all the ways the boy could have been hurt and demanded she apologize. She told Sydney to apologize or go to time-out. Sydney yelled "No!" She did not hurt him, and she would not apologize for not hurting him. It was black and white to her. She could have been persuaded to apologize for throwing the scissors and scaring him, but she was not going to apologize because the scissors *almost* hit him. Her thinking was, *If you hit the person you apologize. If you didn't hit him, you do not have anything to apologize for.* That was logical to her. She was told to go to time-out—and that is when the meltdown ensued.

As Sydney saw it, being punished for this was not OK. Remember the previous year, how she didn't understand the difference between reading silently and reading quietly? It was the same thing this time.

As the teacher approached Sydney, she turned over her chair and bolted from the classroom. The teacher yelled over the intercom for a male backup, because she couldn't leave her students alone. One of the special education teachers put Sydney in a therapeutic hold and being touched escalated the situation.

Now, she was hitting, kicking, spitting, and eventually biting because she didn't want to be touched. She wasn't trying to hurt the teacher. Her motivation was to get away and not be touched, let alone being held tightly against someone else's body with her arms and legs pinned. She was able to get two big bites on the arms of the man who held her.

After all of this happened, I got called to come get her and remove her from the building.

I was told on the phone: "Your daughter has just assaulted another student with a pair of scissors. When she was asked to apologize for bludgeoning the student, she refused to do so. When she was told to go to time-out for disobedience, she was belligerent and violent for no reason. One of our special education teachers had to put her in a therapeutic hold, and while he was holding her she must have bit him thirty times on his arms. Your daughter has a mental illness that we simply cannot handle at this school, and you need to come immediately and pick her up. This incident requires a minimum of a two-day suspension, and we will have to consult the county to see if she is able to remain in a mainstream classroom. Come now, Mrs. Holmes!"

I asked if I could speak with the principal about the punishment for this incident when I came to pick my daughter up. My mind was racing. My heart was pounding. I had such conflicting thoughts. *What am I going to do with this child?*

On the way to pick her up I became livid. As I replayed what the person said on the phone, "She assaulted a student with scissors," I was imagining being sued. I was imagining a child who must have been so badly bludgeoned that he was sent to the hospital by ambulance to have his puncture wounds sewn up. I was sympathizing with this poor teacher who was just trying to help her and was bitten thirty times. Did he have to go to the hospital, too? What would this cost me? How could I face the other parents? I was enraged, ashamed, and feeling inadequate to raise this child. I imagined she could do something that dreadful to her little sister. Was I putting her sibling in danger by keeping her at home?

I called the counselor she had been working with since the closet incident at the previous school. I told her what the school told me, and we discussed the possibility of Sydney being institutionalized. I thought, *If she is this out of control, she needs to be put somewhere where she can be safe and others are safe.* The behavior described to me did seem like mental illness, and she needed something beyond what I could do to help her. Assaulting someone with scissors was way outside the norm of Asperger's Syndrome. The counselor said she would look for some places that took children locally, but I needed to see Sydney and get all the facts from the witnesses before I did anything.

I was feeling so scared as I parked my car. I was so upset thinking about this other child; I had no sympathy for my child. As I walked in, I grew angrier at the school. Why didn't they listen to me? I told them this would happen! Why couldn't they just move her? Why did she have to be forced to use those stupid metal scissors? Did I miss something? Was she mentally ill? I had never ever seen her behave this way at home. She lost control and yelled, but she never behaved this violently.

When I checked in, I bypassed speaking to the principal first and made my way to the classroom. I had been crying and had that swollen eye look. I went to the teacher and begged to know what hospital the other child was in and how to contact his parents so I could apologize and pay their medical bills. I said I was so sorry Sydney assaulted someone, and I began crying again.

The teacher looked at me dumbfounded. She pointed over to where Sydney sat and motioned to the boy still sitting in his desk.

She said, "I don't know what you were expecting, but he wasn't hurt. The scissors didn't even hit him. They grazed him and it scared him, but he's OK."

Now, I looked dumbfounded. What about the aide who was bitten up? Did he have to go to the emergency room? He came over and showed me his arms. He had two bite marks, one on each arm, and neither broke the skin or caused bleeding.

As angry as I was at Sydney for assaulting two people, I was livid with the person who called me and told me the exaggerated story that put me through an emotional nightmare on my ride over. The teacher and the aide told me what happened and that the bigger issue was that she would not apologize. This earned her a two-day suspension? Let me tell you, they were not going to put assault down on her permanent record. Where was the person who called me? She had some 'splainin' to do, Lucy! I had to go get a breather before I assaulted someone. We needed to work this out.

First of all, what actually happened did not warrant a two- to three-day, out-of-school suspension. Second, the words *assault* or *bludgeoning* had better not appear in Sydney's permanent record. I met with the principal and explained that two days at home would feel like a reward to her, not punishment. For ASD kids, out of sight or out of mind is the key. I wanted her to know she was missing playtime and recess and anything fun she liked about school. I suggested a two-day in school suspension. The principal said they didn't have the staff for that. I gladly volunteered to take off work and personally watch Sydney in ISS for two days, so I could take her by the playground and the room at various fun times to show her what she was missing. That way it would be punishment, not a two-day vacation. I asked them to give me a week's worth of schoolwork. I would sit with her those two days, and she would work harder with me in two days than she ever would in a week. She would never want to be suspended like that again, if her brain started to form a plan to get thrown out on purpose. The principal thought it was a great idea and agreed that was what we would do.

I left with Sydney and explained what her next two days of school would be like because of her conduct. At first, she had an "I don't care" attitude. The next day I came with her into the ISS room, and there were stacks of books and worksheets to do.

She said, "That's not fair. I wouldn't do this much school work in a month!" That was the point. I didn't allow her to talk without raising her hand, and she was not allowed to get out of the seat without permission. She could see that I meant business, and she was not having fun. Actual school was more fun than this.

She was getting that point and writing her hand to the bone, when, about halfway through the school day, the principal sent for me. The head of the county's special education division for elementary students decided she needed to intervene on this case.

From that day forward, this horrid woman butted in, and life went downhill. I don't know what her Ph.D. was in, but it certainly was not common sense, and she didn't know much about ASD kids, especially Asperger's. She was probably in her mid-to-late 60's, so she would not have learned about Asperger's and high-functioning autism in her clinical years. She entered the room like she was the almighty expert, and I was the ignoramus mother who needed to learn a thing or two.

Chapter Eight
A Reason for Hope

This expert, this head of special education, said she was overruling Sydney's two-day in-school suspension and was instead calling for a five-day out-of-school suspension, which would result in permanent removal from the school. They cannot call it an expulsion on record, but it was just that. Sydney would be asked to leave this school. Now, because she had an IEP, the county would be required to find another public school in our district that would meet her needs. The head said Sydney was too volatile and dangerous to be around normal children.

I couldn't believe this. Was she joking? Who was this woman who did not know my child, but yet was making such a huge decision concerning her? She claimed to be an expert in ASD, but trust me, she was not.

I called TEACCH and the Autism Society. Both organizations were outraged and agreed that this overstepped a major boundary. An IEP meeting was set where administrators from various schools would come to discuss which school had to take Sydney. I pleaded for consulting on this. Both organizations volunteered to send a representative to argue that moving Sydney was not the right direction. TEACCH was located more an hour from the school, and wound up not being able to get a representative to the meeting, but they faxed a long letter and outline of specifics that would help Sydney stay in a mainstream classroom.

TEACCH insisted that the best course of action for Sydney was to be in a mainstream class with a shadow. The shadow would be there to deal with meltdowns, so the teacher could work with the rest of the class. The Autism Society of North Carolina's representative tried to explain the causes of the meltdowns and reiterated that had Sydney had the scissors and seating that were requested, the event could have been avoided. She was set up to fail.

This meeting was intense. There were fifteen people in the room: that horrid county division head of elementary school special education, who had decided she needed to intervene; the current principal, who had now turned on us; the teacher; three principals from other schools, including Sydney's former public school; the autism advocates; myself; and some others. If I had been in this meeting alone, they would have chewed me up and spit me out. It was obviously slanted in the public school system's favor, and this "expert" division head wanted to see Sydney gone.

The Autism Society advocate knew her stuff. She knew the law, and she didn't let the bigwigs intimidate her one bit. But I felt very intimidated. I felt bullied. The Autism Society representative advocated for my daughter's rights to a free, appropriate, public school education and additional tools to help Sydney be successful at the level she could achieve if she had a proper IEP.

For an hour, people were brought in to testify about Sydney's behaviors and how difficult she made a classroom. Many exaggerated what had happened in order to make their point. They also slanted their comments to make it sound as if she planned those behaviors and was trying to control and manipulate various situations. The district representative said in no way and under no circumstance would the school pay for a shadow for Sydney. She made the motion that Sydney be sent to a specialized, behavior-focused class, often called BEH or BED. The autism advocate strongly opposed it, saying this was not the proper environment for someone on the autism spectrum.

For the next hour, they debated which type of classroom would suit Sydney, the BEH/BED class or a class that was only for autistic children. In both situations, the classroom had five to six students, with three teachers. It would have students in kindergarten through fifth grade. Both had kids with various education issues and challenges. These two classes were my only remaining options. The

Autism Society advocate said that the ASD class, although not the best option, was better than the behavior class. It was the best we could do.

I was so upset. That mean woman was gunning for my daughter, and I didn't understand why. How had Sydney gotten caught in her crosshairs?

And now I had to break the news to Sydney that she would have to leave this school and go to yet another school. As expected, she had a major meltdown. She recalled her feelings for me sometime later, after therapy.

Another new school, she thought. *What did I do this time? I threw my scissors, but they didn't hit anyone. That teacher grabbed me out of my chair, so of course I bit him. Why didn't he get in trouble?*

She didn't want a new school, a new teacher, new kids, new people, and a new routine. That made her very anxious. *Why should I try?* she thought. *Why should I make friends? I'm just going to be kicked out again.* She wanted to stay in this school.

The school allowed themselves five additional days to transition her, making it ten days that she was out of school for the alleged assault.

In the midst of all this, one of my aunts, who lived in Atlanta, asked if my husband and I could come down and volunteer at her ministry event. I needed a distraction, so I welcomed something else to do. This was 2005. Sydney couldn't go to school, and her grandparents were all too happy to have some alone time with her.

The ministry event, which was called the Atlanta Prophecy Conference, provided some spiritual renewal. I went down for prayer, and while the speaker prayed for me, I felt the peace of God, and I needed it. I was hoping for spiritual direction or some words of wisdom pertinent to my situation. None came in that moment, but I at least had peace.

Upon returning home that week, I had a strange dream. In the dream, I was told I would have twin boys, to be named Nathaniel and Zachariah, and a specific time period of October 2007 was given for their births. There was also this "word" that Sydney would receive some form of healing during this same year. I was instructed to share this information with my new pastor. Well, our current pastor wasn't planning on going anywhere that I knew of, so I chalked this dream up to indigestion; but just in case, I wrote it all down, put it in a sealed envelope and taped it to the back of the dresser.

The next day I told Dan, and all he had to hear was twin boys and he was happy. This would be quite the miracle, since I had severe infertility. I had already lost several pregnancies at this point. Sydney healed? Sure. I could believe that. Autism has no known cure. I hadn't really seen God show up or answer my prayers the way I desired, so I could believe I was having twin boys a lot quicker than I could believe Sydney would have any form of healing.

I was curious what the names of the twin boys meant, so I looked them up in the baby book. *Nathaniel* meant "gift from God" or "God has gifted," and *Zachariah* meant "the Lord recalls" or "the Lord remembers." I had no idea what to do with that information, so I did as Mary did in the Bible. I pondered it in my heart, and because 2007 was a definite date, I would know in two years. I at least felt some hope. I wasn't sure what specifically I felt hope about; it was just a feeling I had not felt in a long time. Meanwhile, it was back to reality.

We were now into October of the 2005-2006 school year. The only good thing I could see was that Sydney was at least safe, and her teachers loved her and understood her behavior. I wasn't feeling hopeful. That first day at her new school broke my heart. For the first time in her life, I had to leave her in a classroom while she was kicking and screaming, begging to go home. I cried most of the day. The teachers told me not to worry. They specialized in these types of meltdowns, and they would handle it. I hated to see her so upset, so confused, and so anxious. I hated it!

Sydney's new class had five kids on the spectrum, in kindergarten through grade five. All except Sydney had serious intellectual challenges. One child couldn't speak. Two children weren't toilet trained. One child could repeat back what you said but couldn't initiate her own sentences. And the fifth child had a magnificent memory for TV sermons. T.D. Jakes was his favorite. He could recite an entire sermon. After a week, Sydney was begging to go back to a normal second-grade class because some of the children's behaviors were aggravating her own sensory issues and making her crazy.

Sydney had no one to communicate with other than the teachers. She had no one to play with or to learn social skills with because no child in the room could carry on a conversation. The day was spent mostly finger painting, with little academic work. At first she thought it was a dream. Woo-hoo, no seatwork! Only painting, a few easy worksheets, and playing. Those few worksheets were essentially her academic day. But, after a week, she got bored with this. However, the so-called county expert claimed success. Sydney had no meltdowns, so this was the best fit.

The second week in the new classroom was disastrous. Because the class was more play than structured learning, when the teachers wanted Sydney to do some learning, she didn't want to stop playing. She was asked to put something away and get ready for learning time, and that triggered the biggest meltdown to date. She went through the room like a hurricane, overturning shelves, desks, books, and school supplies. She totally destroyed the room. A teacher assistant took the other children out of the room because it was upsetting to them.

The school called me. They filmed the last bit of the meltdown and what the room looked like, so I could see proof of what Sydney had done. They were not asking her to leave, but they wanted me to see the destruction with my own eyes. I was so embarrassed. In the little bit that I saw of Sydney in action, she looked like a deranged lunatic. I had never seen her behave like that. I had never seen the full capacity of the anger and rage inside of her.

She was not expelled, and I wasn't asked to pay for anything. However, the other students weren't able to go back to the classroom for the rest of the day. I agreed that the punishment should fit the crime, and Sydney should pick up every last thing in that room, even if it took all day and night. They called in her case manager, who stayed in the room with her the next few hours until she did so. It was a long day for her—the caseworker, I mean.

The classroom teachers quickly concluded that this wasn't the best placement for Sydney, but neither was the BED class. They saw how frustrating it would be for her sensory issues if she had to be around some of the students with tics and Tourette's-type noises. They could see she was extremely bright and not being challenged enough in this setting and that she wasn't getting any socialization. They seemed to genuinely care about my daughter, but they were right to be concerned for the safety of the other children. These kids were not used to such a force of nature in their normally placid room.

It was so frustrating. What could I do with Hurricane Sydney? I reflected back to the dream of twin babies and Sydney's healing. After what I saw in that classroom that day, there was no way there was any hope of healing from this situation for any of us.

The Autism Society consultant was finally able to get a shadow for Sydney. We went slowly trying to get her back into the mainstream classroom. A teacher from the ASD class would be her shadow, so we at least had someone Sydney knew and respected. The school wanted to ease her into the class that would be the least stressful, so we would begin with the specials like PE, art, music, and Spanish. If she could contain her meltdowns in the ASD class, she would get to go to the fun classes, as long as she was accompanied by the shadow. She would then go to recess and lunch with the other students.

In the beginning, she did one-fourth of the school day in the mainstream classroom with the shadow, then one-half, then three-fourths, and then finally the whole day. She was succeeding! The shadow worked solely with Sydney, helping her stay on task and avoid meltdowns. Should one occur, the shadow would deal with it, and the teacher could keep moving forward with the rest of the class. The shadow developed verbal and hand signals to help Sydney communicate when she was anxious, and, during these times, they would go for a walk, get water, or make some deliveries to other classes. These diversions brought Sydney's anxiety down, and she could get back to focusing in class with minimal disruption to the other students.

She had four or five major meltdowns in the coming weeks, but the shadow handled them without having to call me, and Sydney was making friends in the classroom. I wasn't called to school to deal with her for the rest of the school year! In fact, she was one of the top students academically in the mainstream class. She loved her teacher, she was happy in the class, and she really loved her shadow. She began to like this school and to feel accepted there.

The Autism Society of North Carolina was a huge help during this year. Before Sydney was transferred into the room permanently, a representative from the society came and explained autism and sensory integration issues to the class so the other students could better understand what they might see or experience with Sydney. Having someone explain the situation to her classmates on their level was a major help in Sydney feeling included in the class.

Sydney's anxiety was always high, but she and her counselor were working on ways to manage it. Her counselor was also helping her with anger and frustration, and at the end of the school year, she was given an award from the county for being the school system's most-improved student. The year ended on a positive note. Sydney was even invited back for the next year. She would get to go to the same school for third grade. The principal told her at the end of the year: "We love you so much, girl. We want to keep you around until fifth grade!" The special education teachers loved her as well. It felt like we had finally found the answer. Hopefully, we would have smooth sailing for the rest of elementary school.

Chapter Nine
Therapy Mom

In addition to the protocols with Sydney, our second daughter, Erica, had her own challenges. Her issues added to the weight on my shoulders and the stress that continued to influence my decision about having other children. Thankfully, Erica's Diagnosis Day was not as severe as Sydney's. Erica was born at thirty-six and one-half weeks. She wasn't a preemie baby, though, because she weighed eight pounds, four ounces.

Before she was even one year old, Erica had multiple ear infections. She was so sweet that she wouldn't really cry until the infection escalated to a double ear infection and required medical attention. She was constantly on antibiotics. When her teeth came in, they looked horrible. They were different sizes and shapes, and some teeth never came. Her mouth looked like Quasimodo. I started to wonder if this was the effect of the medicine I had taken in order to keep the pregnancy.

Everything with Erica was delayed. She began to roll over and grasp things pretty early, but she didn't walk until she was fifteen or sixteen months. When she learned to crawl, it was backward. Sydney had begun talking around age one; Erica, not a peep. She began to say words around age two, but we couldn't understand them. The doctor said, "Oh, the second child is sometimes delayed; and besides, you're used to Sydney the Wonder Kid doing everything early."

My gut said something was wrong. Some facts from early

development psychology class were coming back to me, and I was getting concerned that she was mentally challenged. She knew her name, but often when I said it, there was no response, just a blank stare and a sweet smile. As she approached age three, her verbal skills were still lacking and her gross motor skills were behind. I was starting to worry about autism and mental retardation, which was now called *intellectual challenges*. The doctor didn't feel she needed any evaluations, so I found a clinic that did free assessments, and that was another difficult day.

The first test was a hearing screening. Problem number one: Erica could only hear three of the four tones. The screening showed the ear drum was stationary and not moving the sound into the ear. The sounds were bouncing out. She heard the fourth tone, which is the lower one, so the assessors felt that she could finish the screening if they spoke lower and louder.

It turned out her fine motor skills were very advanced and her intelligence was actually slightly above average. However, in addition to her hearing issue, she showed sensory aversions, speech delay, and delayed gross motor skills. The assessors felt more testing was needed, as she could also be diagnosed with "pervasive development disorder, not otherwise specified" (PDDNOS), which at that time was considered to be on the autism spectrum. We began a search for therapists and screenings for Erica, as well.

She, too, saw a geneticist, neurologist, ENT, OT, PT, and speech pathologist. The ENT said step one was getting her hearing repaired. She had surgery to have tubes inserted, which is commonplace, but when they got in to do the tubes, they found she had "glue ear," meaning that the eardrum was stuck in place and causing her inability to hear. They repaired her ear and said it was a good thing we got this taken care of because it would greatly aid in her speech therapy.

Erica already had sensory issues, but now it was as if she had been hearing everything under water, and with her hearing intact and the eardrum functioning, everything seemed very loud, and it was distressing to her.

But at least now that Erica could hear, we could move to step two: speech therapy. She was about 40 percent delayed. Not only did she need to catch up on her vocabulary, but the few words she did know, she had been hearing incorrectly, so she had to have "special instruction" therapy and essentially learn every word and concept over again. For example, she called *apple* by its last syllable alone, "pull," and *purple* by its last syllable, so if she said "pull" we didn't know if she meant the fruit, the color, or a toy she called a "pull." She had speech therapy two or three times a week. She had special instruction therapy twice a week. She had OT once a week for the sensory issues. We couldn't afford PT to help with the gross motor skills, so she and I started taking a Mommy and Me gymnastics and movement class. It was cheaper than PT, it gave us time to be together, and she loved it. She had so much therapy that we needed some fun time. It took about nine months to get her close to developmental level.

However, having one child on the spectrum, I was concerned that Erica had ASD as well. I made an appointment with TEACCH to have her evaluated. It took a while to get her in, but her diagnosis came back PDDNOS and mild ADD. Erica struggles with focus, sensory, and handling big emotions, but her temperament was quite different than her sister's. She was easy going and loved school, and school loved her. Once we got out of the toddler age and got her developmentally on target, she began to soar. She had her issues, but Sydney was the squeaky wheel. They each had some form of therapy every day, so between the two I was always carting one of them to therapy and entertaining the other one during the therapy. Instead of being the soccer mom, I was the therapy mom, meaning as a counselor, I couldn't really perform therapy. I needed therapy!

Chapter Ten
Two Steps Forward ...

Sydney made some great gains during the summer between second and third grade. She made some friends at church, plus two friends from the previous school year kept in touch over the summer. Her anxiety seemed manageable, and her meltdowns were fewer and fewer. It felt like things were looking up. The school contacted me before the academic year began to tell me they were doing something unprecedented to help her. Because she ended second grade with measurable success and had some good progress with her shadow, the school had a wonderful plan for third grade. The principal asked the second grade teacher to move up to third grade. The class would be made up of 80 percent of the kids from the previous school year, which would mean less change for Sydney. She would start the year in the mainstream class, and this year the class would be in a room in the building, not a trailer! And she would start with a shadow.

The school was going above and beyond to help her. Third grade was going to be the best school year ever! Sydney would be so successful and maybe not even need a shadow by the end of the year. This was tremendous, particularly as I was taking on more responsibility at my job at the private school. I could finally take on teaching a high school psychology class, because I might actually get to stay at work every day. Imagine a school year without the constant phone calls from school. Talk about some pie in the sky expectations. I started the new school year with so much hope.

But at orientation we learned that the woman who had shadowed Sydney the previous year was in the restaurant business now. A new shadow would be assigned. I didn't know at the time that this shadow wasn't trained in ASD or SPD, or in Sydney's background, or even in special education. She essentially had been told that Sydney was high-spirited and high-maintenance. The school told me that the new shadow had experience with various behavior issues, but I found out later that her own child had conduct issues, and that's the experience the school was relying on. I tried to stay positive. Sydney had a great teacher, she would be in a mainstream class, and she at least had some support with the new shadow.

I'm not sure how things began to unravel so quickly. It's not really anyone's fault. I had let myself believe Sydney would start this school year building on the previous year. I forgot about the two-step backward principle that tends to affect her.

Could some things have been different? Yes. But was anyone to blame? No. I think we all had our expectations too high. The principal thought with all of the new tools in place Sydney couldn't possibly fail. Her teacher, who had questioned the autism diagnosis from the beginning, seemed to think Sydney just needed to be around normal kids, and then she would be normal. I think we all thought that her progress meant that her Asperger's had completely disappeared over the summer or something. We all seemed to think the cute, blonde-haired, blue-eyed girl was going to show up as a neuro-typical third-grader, so excited to start back to school with a heart full of love for learning.

Things began to spiral downward when the school felt as if Sydney needed to be weaned from her shadow. I wasn't aware that the shadow wasn't with her all of the time. The IEP did not specify that she should be weaned. It said she had the shadow for the full year. But the school began to see the shadow as a crutch for Sydney, and they started using the shadow as a teacher assistant in nearby classes. Sydney's anxiety level shot back up and her meltdowns returned. She began to develop a nasty habit of refusal behaviors such as breaking her pencils, shredding her clothing, chewing her hair, and running out of the classroom when she was confused about an assignment or classroom directive. If she thought the work was too hard or too boring, she would refuse to do it.

To the adults in the room, this refusal behavior looked like disrespect and outright disobedience. They saw Sydney as oppositional defiant and not as an ASD child. The teacher began to say more and more that she did not think this was ASD but ODD. She saw the refusal behavior as a tantrum, not a cry for help. She became determined to prove that Sydney didn't have ASD but instead just needed firm discipline. In other words, if everybody would simply treat Sydney like they treated every other child, she would become normal.

I found out later through Sydney's therapist that what appeared to be anger and defiance was really anxiety, boredom, or frustration with her body and mind for not doing what she thought it should. Can you imagine what it's like for a child who is biologically eight years old to have the mind or intelligence of a ten-year-old, but the emotional instability of a five-year-old and be trapped in a body with the motor skills of a six-year-old? Add to all of this the stress of sensory processing issues and you have an explosion waiting to happen.

When Sydney acted out in the mainstream class, she was placed in the ASD class for discipline, but she saw it as punishment. Her teachers would warn her that if she couldn't act like a third-grader, she would have to go back to the ASD classroom. They were trying to give her incentive to "act right." However, placing her in the ASD room only served to disrupt two classrooms each day. She found the autistic children in the secluded class frustrating. To be in that room was now a "diss" to her. She saw it as humiliation, and she would escalate if she were sent out of the main classroom to the ASD class.

Foreign language and P.E. were disastrous. I could just about count on getting a call every day during those times. Sometimes, I was asked to come calm her down, so she could stay the rest of the day. But, eventually, I was asked to come get her. In late fall, there were whispers that she might not be able to stay in the mainstream classroom. By Christmas break, I was being called at least twice a week, in the middle of the day. She was unraveling. Once the meltdown hit, there seemed to be no point of return and the second half of the day was shot. Do you know what this meant? Meetings, discussions, experts, and more meetings!

Could she stay in the mainstream class? That would be the question of the year. We knew she could not be mainstreamed without a shadow; however, this year the shadow was not as much of a resource as the previous year. We had tried the ASD classroom, and that wasn't a fit. What else was left to try? I felt like the school did really want it to work, but we were running out of options. It was decided that because she seemed to lose control after lunch, we would come get her at lunch every day or be available to come calm her down and refocus her on school work. We also decided that PE and Spanish weren't working and the effort to get her to participate in these classes wasn't worth it. She could use the time with the shadow to catch up on work, to walk, or to have quiet time. Dan asked his boss if he could use his vacation time for a few weeks to attend school with Sydney. His boss graciously agreed.

Dan knew I needed a break from all of this, and he could work at school while monitoring Sydney's behavior in the classroom. The school was gracious to let Dan attend school with Sydney. We call this the year Dan had to repeat third grade.

In January and February, Dan and Sydney headed off to school. Dan sat at the back of the room with his laptop, working and watching, then he left at lunch. This gave me a half-day of uninterrupted work. If Sydney had a tantrum or was refusing to work and the shadow couldn't engage her, Dan did. He would then return to his laptop. If a call came after lunch, I would get her from school and bring her back to my office with me. This worked beautifully for a while, and we again thought we had found a working solution. But by the end of January, just about as soon as Dan would leave, the school would call asking me to come get her. It started out once a week, then twice, then gradually every day. By early February, I just decided it was easier and less stressful to go get her when Dan left.

February 2007: Winds of Change

Remember the dream that I would have twins by October 2007? Yep, I was pregnant. At this stage, I was the mother of two special-needs children, as well as being a high school guidance counselor, a professional counselor, and the teacher of a high school psychology class. I was juggling all of that while running back and forth to my third-grader's school at least twice a week to either deal with her at school, or bring her back to work with me. Plus, both of my daughters had a therapy session each day.

A few times when I picked up Sydney, I had to sneak her into my psychology class where she kept a watchful eye on students breaking the rules. She acted as if she was the second teacher. She learned the students' names, wrote down anyone who acted up and what the infraction was, and then gave me the detailed report at the end of class. If we were writing or doing something on the board, she pointed out poor handwriting, spelling issues, grammar errors, and whom she felt had behavior issues. My students enjoyed having her, but I did not. I was probably breaking a rule myself having her in the classroom. This was, in fact, the school that had expelled her in first grade, but what was I to do?

The proverbial handwriting was slowly appearing on the wall. The public school was making noise that they didn't want to keep Sydney. Dan couldn't continue to go to third grade; he needed to work. I couldn't continue to pick up Sydney after lunch and sneak her into my classroom. Oh, and I was trying to get excited about my pregnancy, but I was fearful of having another special-needs child. The estimated due date was October 27. Life was too overwhelming. Isn't there a verse somewhere about not getting more than we can bear or handle? Sydney and Erica were elated; they just knew this baby would be a brother.

The dreaded call came late that February. The head of the special education division for the county, the woman we called "Demonica," called to set up a special meeting to discuss where Sydney would finish third grade. Not only did she not believe that Sydney had Asperger's Syndrome, but she also explained: "Mrs. Holmes, you need to come to terms with the fact that your daughter is mentally ill, and you and your husband may not be suited to provide for her needs."

I am ashamed of the thoughts that ran through my head. As a Christian, I cannot print the reply that first came to mind in response to that awful indictment of my daughter.

The woman proceeded to say she had "checked out some alternatives" for Sydney. She had looked into a day treatment center, and at the meeting she suggested that Sydney be placed in this facility. At this institution, she would receive treatment, education, and medication. If we could not afford this facility, we could "terminate our parental rights and hand her over as a ward of the state," and then she would get this fabulous facility for free. If we gave up our rights, she could go into the system, be put on Medicaid, and the state could provide the care she would need.

I exploded!

"What kind of an idiot do you think I am that I would willingly give up custody of my child and hand her over as a ward of the state?" I asked. I was adamant that Sydney was not mentally ill; professionals at TEACCH had diagnosed her with Asperger's Syndrome, and under no circumstances did I want this "option" brought up in a formal IEP meeting or to go on the record. I was adamant that I did not see this as a viable option and did not wish to further discuss it. Ever!

She proceeded to tell me that my child was not only a burden to the school and the school district she was placed in, but she also was a burden to the entire county. She asked if I would consider homeschooling Sydney to relieve the county of this heavy burden. I am not exaggerating; this was the conversation that took place.

I think I retorted in a smart-alecky tone something to the affect of, "If you do not deem me capable of raising my own child, why are you suggesting I educate her? I thought you represented the almighty public school system and special education department that holds all the answers!" The conversation soon ended. She did set up a meeting for early March to discuss Sydney's placement into yet another school.

I was losing what little patience I had with the school system. Their inability to follow the IEP, to manage Sydney's behaviors at school, and their daily disruption of my work schedule was weighing on me. In addition, my trust that the Lord would take care of this was not looking promising. I decided it was up to me to handle it all. Even with two incomes, our finances were strained. We had spent thousands of dollars on both our children's treatment and care. Money was tight or non-existent all the time. Daily life was just stressful. I was constantly awaiting the call to "Come get your child." And now we awaited what would be said or decided in that upcoming March IEP meeting. Certainly, I will be rescued, I thought. Certainly, I will be defended or protected. Sydney had rights. I had rights. Sydney was not the only autistic child in the world that school systems needed to address, right? Surely, God would do something. I was at my maximum capacity for stress and daily maintaining. Surely, it could not get worse.

It did. The last Sunday in February, I began to feel painful cramps while singing at church. It was during the standing portion of the song service, so I decided to sit. The pain got worse. I excused myself to the foyer and called my doctor. He said I needed rest and to come in Monday. I was bound and determined to stay positive and not think the worst. After all, the way I saw it, God owed me. I mean, look at my life and what I dealt with on a daily basis. He was going to pull through and take care of this one. This was an easy one for God. I returned to my chair in the sanctuary and passionately joined the congregation in singing the song, "Rescue." What a perfect song! I needed to be rescued!

The cramps continued, followed by bleeding. My brain was screaming at me, "You are miscarrying again!" I was at war with my mind.

"No! God would not allow that to happen to me! I had that dream, that Word. In October 2007, I am to have twins. No doubt. He has to take care of this!" I had not even wanted another pregnancy. I was done with the miscarrying and emotional pain of all that. This was God's idea, His timetable, and He needed to fix it! I had already endured seven or eight miscarriages in my life. My life was already a nightmare. God would not do this to me, too?

So, I kept claiming that this was not a miscarriage. I claimed that everything would be OK on Monday. I kept thanking and praising God and claiming that He would come through.

Dan was amazed at my resilience. He typically calls me a pessimist, although I refer to myself as a realist. I wanted Dan at the doctor appointment with me to hear the news that everything would be OK. He was feeling positive because I was so positive. I was holding on to the dream and that October 27 date! I stood firm. I spoke to that mountain and told it to be moved as good Christians said I should do. My faith was at an all-time high. This was going to be a non-issue. Period.

On Monday, the doctor couldn't find a heartbeat. That worried me, but then I thought: *Hey, God can handle this! Doctors do not get the final word. Their machines could be wrong.*

We walked out of the office and Dan said, "I really think this is going to be OK, if you're not worried about it." I made some comments about maybe homeschooling Sydney in the fall. After all, I couldn't work and take care of a baby or babies. It would work out.

But by Wednesday, the miscarriage was happening. I called the doctor. They had been taking my blood and checking various hormone levels. The levels were dropping. They said that they were sorry. The doctor suggested I stay home and stay close to a restroom.

I was in total shock. Then the trauma, and I apologize for being graphic, when the miscarriage happened. When I looked into the toilet, there were two fetuses in sacs. Babies. I saw two!

I lost it. I called the doctor to report what had happened. He asked me to come in to check my blood work and see if a D and C would need to be performed, as well.

I asked, "What do I do with the babies?"

The doctor callously replied, "Just flush the fetuses down the toilet."

I broke down and was hyperventilating. Each time I walked over to flush the toilet, I saw the two embryo sacs and would almost vomit. I couldn't do it. My heart cried, *God, where are you?* It took hours for me to flush that toilet. When I pushed the toilet handle, my joy, hope, and faith were flushed away with those two little sacs. God had failed me.

I snapped. I said to Him, "I am D-O-N-E! Do you hear me? Done!" My thoughts were racing, and my faith was below zero. I thought and may even have said aloud: "You heal me so that I can conceive, only to give me a child that I specifically said I could not handle. I said 'No Autism! No life-altering disabilities!' You said you give perfect gifts. Every gift from You is supposed to be perfect. This gift is a little defective! Did you not remember I have already had several miscarriages?"

I was done trying. I had made peace and cried and come to terms with not having any more children.

What in the world was that dream about having twins? I didn't ask to be pregnant. I did not want to be pregnant. My life was moving forward.

"What are You doing? Are you aware of what is going on here God? I don't know what is worse—believing that you are distant and do not know what I am going through, or believing you know, that you see all of this, and you simply **do not care**!"

Oh no, that stupid IEP meeting was that week, too. I called the head lady with the county office, explained what had happened, and requested a change of date. I explained that I might even need a surgical procedure, and if I could put the meeting off a few more weeks, that would be most helpful.

She snapped at me and curtly informed me how inconvenient that would be for her. And more than a dozen people were to be present, and asking to change the date was very inconsiderate. Miscarriages happen all the time, she said, and if I was too stressed out to attend the meeting, they could have it without me.

Are you kidding me? Why would I allow the fate of my daughter's education to be decided without me, knowing this woman wanted my daughter placed in an institution outside of my care? Could anyone be more rude? It dawned on me that this woman not only did not care for my daughter, she certainly did not care for me. I knew I was not able to handle an intense IEP meeting, especially one of this emotional magnitude, and I insisted the meeting date be moved. She impatiently agreed.

My stress and emotions were at an all-time high, and my faith was at an all-time low. Call it hormones, bad parenting, bad school system—who knows—but Sydney got suspended that very week. I was called again to come pick her up from school. No rest for the weary.

I had a terrible mommy moment that I wish I could erase. I informed Sydney that she was ruining my life. The stress of having to constantly pick her up at school and deal with her school behavior was more than likely a major factor in my miscarriage. Living every day with the fear that the school would call me was too hard, and I could not handle any more stress!

Her face fell, and she suddenly had the saddest expression I had ever seen. She looked at me with big, remorseful eyes and said: "Do you mean I killed my baby brother?"

"Yes, you did!" I answered, angrily. She sat in complete silence the entire car ride home.

For years to come, I heard her say, "My mommy miscarried her baby because I stressed her out. I killed the baby." Every time she said it, my heart would break and remind me of that horrible moment when my stress took over my good sense.

Well, I was on a roll. I just continued to spew the venom. It was coming out, and anyone near me could be sprayed with it at any time. Everyone would be getting their fair share at some point. I'd had it, and everyone needed to know it. Forget about denial, sadness, disappointment, or bargaining—I was just plain angry.

As I was writing this portion of the book, reliving the pain and hating what I had said, I was waiting for Sydney's middle school band to perform. I sat in awe of God's faithfulness, despite my anger and disapproval of Him and His plans for me. How did I doubt God? Why was I so angry then? I realized that this is what people feel when they don't have hope. At that moment, with the miscarriage and another school suspension for Sydney, all hope was lost. I didn't see how anything could improve. But, now, here I sat at this concert, about to see my daughter perform, full of pride for her and awe of my God and His faithfulness to me. The popular song, "Blessed be the Name," sung by the contemporary Christian group Tree 63, came to mind. The song is based on Job 1:21 when Job said, "He gives and takes away." Years ago, I had hated that song and that blasted song, "Rescue." Whenever I heard either of them at church or any other gathering, I would bolt for the door and wait out the song service in the ladies' room. If one of them came on the radio, I shut it off. These songs—daggers to my heart and soul in the midst of my pain—now bring me comfort.

The weekend after the miscarriage, my in-laws offered to take the girls to the mountains to give Dan and me some time and space to talk and grieve. We needed to process the loss of the twins, the loss of dreams. We needed to think about the upcoming IEP meeting, Sydney's academic future, everything. My mother-in-law saw that I needed respite from ASD for a weekend.

Dan and I spent the weekend mostly in silence. I had cried, screamed, and asked why. Now, I was just numb and bitter. One night, I heard gentle crying beside me. Dan's not one to cry often, so I knew something was wrong. I asked if he was OK, and he began to spill out his feelings and disappointments.

Dan had already envisioned himself at T-ball games, Little League, and Royal Ranger campouts (our church's version of Boy Scouts). He was mourning what would never be.

While he was in the early stage of grief, I had moved past sadness to resentment toward God. Dan, although sad and pensive, never doubted God one day. He remained faithful to God while I was on the verge of jumping off the faith cliff. For the rest of the weekend, we cried together and he held me.

Later, I was so thankful Dan was solid in his faith and never let go of his hope, but at the time, I was very angry with him for siding with God. I saw his loyalty to God as disloyalty to me. I know that's twisted thinking, but when bitterness and resentment get inside your heart, your thinking is not godly and clear.

Soon, the dreaded IEP meeting arrived. About a dozen people had gathered to decide the educational fate of our daughter. Dan decided that he should come; he wasn't sure if I would be able to curb my tongue with Demonica present. I also liked to call her "Cruella DeVil" because it felt like she was after my Dalmatian puppy. That is how I explained it to Sydney, oftentimes.

The meeting began with the principal of her current school, the assistant principal, her teacher, the special education teacher, and the county's elementary special education head all up to bat for the school. For Sydney, there was an advocate for me, an autism specialist, Dan, me, and some others. The special education teacher, whom I did like and did believe cared for our daughter, began the meeting stating that the school could no longer meet Sydney's needs and suggesting she be placed elsewhere.

Demonica took the floor and began the conversation I had forbid her to start when we talked by phone. She commenced to say on the record that as a psychologist, she believed Sydney to be mentally ill. She began to lay out her plan for institutionalization in the day treatment program.

My mind said, "Oh, no, she didn't!" I'm sure my face registered my displeasure. I slowly began to rise out of my chair to tell this woman on the other side of the table that I was not in agreement.

Dan gently, but firmly, pressed my leg down under the table and sat me back down. "It's not worth it," he whispered.

I regained some composure and repeated what I had said on the phone earlier. "This is not an option." I mentioned that she had called me with this diabolical plan, and I had specifically told her it was not an option and should not be mentioned in the formal setting.

Sydney's regular classroom teacher, who had suggested another placement, vouched for her and agreed that a day treatment facility was not the best solution. Slowly, other teachers who knew Sydney chimed in and agreed.

Demonica's ego was a little deflated, but she firmly said, "Then, there is only one option left." She then turned our attention to teachers from two other schools in the district.

These teachers represented schools with behavior-focused programs or BED/BEH classrooms, and one of the teachers was the one who had helped lock Sydney in the time-out closet back in first grade. I was not sure if that time-out closet had been dismantled or not, but no way!

First, I had promised my daughter she would never, ever have to return to that school. Second, I still worked forty-five minutes away from the school, and it was too disruptive to my work schedule to drive that far to rescue teachers. This was her assigned school, based on where we lived, so they were pressing for her to attend school there. However, the second school with the BEH/BED option was closer to my workplace and my mom's house. It was not what I wanted for Sydney, but it was the lesser of the two evils.

I sat there wondering, *How did we get here?* I was disappointed with God. How could this possibly be the best for Sydney? Didn't He care about her education and my sanity? This seemed unfair on so many levels.

Chapter Eleven
BREAKTHROUGH

This chapter is where I might lose some readers, and you may think I have lost my mind or exaggerated details to make the story more interesting. However, I committed to write the truth of what I saw, heard, and felt. So, remember that I warned you.

Sydney was placed in the behavior-focused classroom. Her teacher was an ex-cop from New York who had once worked with juvenile delinquents, children with some form of behavioral disorder. She was tough, but Demonica said this teacher had a 100 percent rate of getting kids back to the mainstream classroom. She slyly said, under her breath almost, that Sydney might ruin that record.

The teacher was in her third trimester of pregnancy, and I was told she had issues with previous pregnancies. I wondered why in the world she was working in a behavior-focused classroom if she had a high-risk pregnancy. Our daughter's violent meltdowns and a pregnant teacher did not seem like a good match to me, but the teacher kept assuring me that she could handle Sydney.

Sydney started out like a wild horse bucking at being in a new stable. She tested her boundaries, but the school handled it and the daily phone calls stopped—until a horrible day in April when I was called to come get her. When I arrived at her classroom, Sydney was isolated in a corner. I wasn't sure what was more concerning, the extremely hateful look on her face, or the rug burn from her chin to her forehead.

It was the teacher's birthday, and someone had brought flowers for her in a glass vase. Sydney had been asked to do a compliance task, and she refused. She was told to go to time-out and, again, did not comply. Instead, she walked up to the teacher's desk, grabbed the vase of flowers, and threw it to the floor. She then tried to hit the teacher in the stomach, while screaming that she wanted to kill the teacher's baby.

The teacher proudly described for me how she subdued Sydney and got her "under control." She and her assistant took Sydney to the floor, cop-style, facedown into the carpet, arms behind her back. One of them pressed a knee into her back, and her face was rubbed into the floor until she relented and stopped fighting.

I felt a wave of emotions, the strongest one, shock. Could Demonica be right? Could Sydney be bipolar or have some other mental issue? This behavior seemed outrageous for what I had read and studied about Asperger's.

I began to ponder a phrase from Scripture, from John 10:10. The thief comes to "steal, kill, and destroy." It kept coming to my mind, and I wondered how my beautiful, blonde, slender-framed child could have the strength and state of mind to steal the flowers from the teacher's desk, destroy the vase, and threaten to kill the teacher's baby. What was this? What in the world could motivate such behavior? Sydney had never been around physical violence of any kind. We heavily monitored what she watched on television, and Bob and Larry and the Disney Princesses certainly did not model such behavior. Where was this rage coming from?

Sydney was growing up in church. How could God allow a child to be spiritually attacked? She was supposed to be covered under the spiritual protection of her father and me. How could she fight back? Did she even understand what was going on in her mind?

Sydney's behavior began to escalate after that day. As long as the teachers had handled everything, her tactics had not been so severe, but when she saw they would call me, her behavior went into overdrive.

Years later, she reflected on that third-grade year, including the months before she transferred. *Maybe they don't like me*, she thought about the previous school. *They were just pretending. I cannot trust anyone.*

Then the behavior-focused class with the ex-cop teacher: *Why does she upset me on purpose? Why does she tear up my work and tell me to start over, and expect me not to be upset? I need to just work quickly so she won't tear it up, and I don't have time to do it over. If I get an answer wrong, will she hurt me? Will she pull me out of my chair? I shouldn't ask the teacher questions.*

At this point, we did agree to see the child psychiatrist again and work with medications. I felt like we had tried everything else. I was not opposed to medicine, but Sydney was so small and so young. She was only in third grade, but the medicines the psychiatrist put her on were heavy hitters. She started out with Zoloft, which did help her anxiety some, but when they upped her dosage, it seemed to make her fearless and far too brave. Her inhibitions moved in the wrong direction.

Instead of lowering the Zoloft dosage, the doctors added Abilify to stabilize her mood. When Abilify didn't work, they replaced it with Depakote. Depakote and Abilify are often used in bipolar disorder or other mental disturbances that disrupt mood. Because of her aggressive behavior, an anti-psychotic drug called Risperdal was added. With all these medicines, Sydney wasn't eating or sleeping well. She had always been a great eater and would put herself to bed without any fuss. She knew when she was hungry and when she was sleepy. The medicines were making things much worse, and her behavior at school hadn't changed.

When I brought this up with the psychiatrist, the solution was to add another medication for sleep. No! Sydney was already on too many medications, and the side effects were far outweighing the benefits. In fact, we really didn't see any benefits. She was like a zombie. Her dad had already said that he would rather her be out of control than drugged out of her mind. Sydney would often tell me she couldn't feel anything anymore—sadness, happiness, excitement, nothing. She was still angry; the medicine simply kept her too tired to act out.

While dealing with all of this, I was still grieving the miscarriage of the twins. I was juggling my job, mothering this out-of-control child, managing therapies for a second child who had her own learning issues, and our finances were strained. I was no longer just disappointed in God, I was furious. I was a woman scorned, and I was realizing that the "Name it and claim it" teaching I had been under in my younger years was not theologically sound. According to this philosophy, if you were a Christian and you were obedient to God, you would only walk in blessings and would not suffer. You could name your blessings and, if you had enough faith, God would make them happen. I was disillusioned and angry. I felt betrayed by God. Maybe this Christianity thing wasn't for me after all. Maybe I would have better results on my own.

The situation with Sydney was causing undue stress on our extended family. Her grandparents didn't like seeing their grandchild with a rug burn all over her face. They didn't enjoy seeing her become a spaced-out, lifeless zombie.

My dad had begun to experience a personal revival of faith. He commenced to pray for Sydney. I don't mean he said a little prayer here and there. He prayed intently for Sydney's behavior and for her to be delivered from this ordeal. I was at my wit's end. I had stopped praying. I simply existed. I, too, felt like a zombie, only I had no medications to blame it on. I just felt lifeless inside. My joy count was zero. I had nothing to look forward to anymore. Life was too hard, and God was not helping. I'm glad someone was praying. God obviously had not listened to my prayers, and He obviously didn't love me. I was living in my own personal hell on earth. I could see no hope; I could see no way things would get better.

My angst and lack of hope grew to despair. Was something else going on with Sydney besides Asperger's? I just could not understand her violent behavior. It seemed like she was two people. We didn't see these violent behaviors at home. She got into trouble at church occasionally around transition times, but she was never violent. School was the only place this violence seemed appear.

What if this behavior did manifest at home? What if Sydney turned on her little sister? Erica was only three years old, and I kept having nightmares of Sydney hurting her. What would I do if this happened? Out of fear, I asked Sydney's therapist to research placement options should I be forced to make such a choice.

God, where are you? I asked. *Are you seeing this? Are you aware of the torment and pain I am in? Oh, that's right, I'm doing this on my own now.* My husband saw me falling apart. His prayer life got stronger, while mine faded into oblivion. My dad prayed for Sydney, and my husband was praying for me. I was unraveling, and Sydney was more and more out of control. The doctor's comments that the stress probably contributed to my miscarriage were not helping. I was beginning to have some not-so-motherly thoughts toward Sydney. Life seemed bleak and dark.

The dream I'd had about the twins also suggested that I tell my new pastor, which seemed strange at the time, but since then, a new pastor had indeed come to the church. In my despair, I called him to say that I would no longer be on the prayer team at church. Because God didn't hear me, I should, therefore, not be praying for other people, I told him, especially as I wasn't sure I even believed all that stuff, anymore. In fact, I said, maybe I should quit counseling altogether. I wasn't sure if I even wanted to continue attending church because I would just be faking it.

My pastor said, "Stephanie, I think you do need to take a break from some ministerial duties, but I'm worried about you. I think you need to come in, and let's talk about this."

I did meet with him, albeit reluctantly. I was expecting a lecture about faith and how God is good and for him to ask me how I could think this way. I just knew he was going to tell me to snap out of it.

I was pleasantly surprised when he gave me permission to speak my mind. He didn't correct me or my theology. He listened! No lectures, no advice, he just let me vent.

The pastor asked me not to make important decisions when I was so upset. He recommended that I take some time to figure out what I did and did not believe. He had preached a sermon about forgiveness the previous week, and he talked about the empty chair technique. Empty chair is a counseling technique where you imagine the person who has hurt you sitting in a chair in front of you, and you simply tell them how you feel. You say what you want, and you vent.

I told the pastor sarcastically that I wished I could put God in the empty chair and put Him on trial, or write Him a nasty letter.

He said calmly: "God already knows how you feel. Maybe you should write a letter to Him and don't hold anything back. Remember, He already knows."

Hmmm, I thought, *I would love an opportunity to tell God how I felt. I could do that.*

My Christian upbringing prohibits the Christian from questioning God. You don't get angry with Him. You don't ask why. I tried several times to write the letter, but it kept sounding so spiritual and not at all what I was feeling. But, finally, I let it rip. One angry page after another began to flow. I had no idea all of that was inside me. I accused God of being a child-abuser and said that I wished I could call the Department of Social Services on Him for His spiritual mishandling of me. I ranted that as an earthly parent, I would do anything to keep my child from suffering. If I could heal Sydney, I would. But He could and chose not to. I was raising my fist at God and demanding answers. I felt empowered and angrier.

I emailed the letter to my pastor. I don't think he was ready for such a vile, angry letter to God. Again, he suggested we talk; and again, no judgment, no debates. He simply listened. What it came down to in our discussions was that I couldn't reach a point where I doubted the existence of God. I had seen too much in my life for that. So, I was stuck with a mean God who existed, but who did not help me and did not hear me crying out.

My pastor suggested that since I needed to discover what I believed about God, I should do a little research and study the character and nature of God.

"Good," I said. "I'm starting with the Old Testament where He sent fire and brimstone and flood and killed people!"

The pastor didn't roll his eyes; he simply suggested I include the New Testament and asked me to check in occasionally and let him know how I was doing. I agreed.

I knew I could approach this through an educational, cognitive process, as if I were doing research. This was a long process. While I was on this search for truth, evidence hard to believe came to light.

I was not at my best place spiritually, but Dan's faith seemed not to waver. He became more resolved to pray and seek answers. He went the next step and began to pray over Sydney's room, including her windows and doors. He asked me to help him anoint the room with olive oil. He anointed the doorframes, windows, her bed, and furniture, and he asked God to protect her mind and help her through this difficult time. He asked for wisdom to parent her.

That same month, the last month of the school year, I got a call from my dad. He didn't offer much chitchat; he asked me a strange question: "Stephanie, how did Sydney sleep last night?"

That's an odd question, I thought; and, honestly, I didn't really care at the moment. But he was insistent that I ask her.

"Okay, let me find her," I sighed. "Sydney! Come here. Pawpaw needs to know how you slept last night."

She looked at me curiously, as if she were wondering why in the world he would call to ask that question. She said sheepishly, "Good, I guess."

So I told my dad, "She said, 'Good.'"

His reply was interesting: "I was worried she'd be woken up by the spiritual warfare in her room last night. I'm glad she was able to sleep. OK, that's all I needed to know."

I was in a hurry and didn't have time to ask the question I was thinking at that moment, so we hung up. Five minutes later, Sydney came into my room as I was getting ready for work.

"Why did you ask me how I was sleeping?" she asked.

I answered, "Your pawpaw needed to know that, so he called and asked for some reason."

She said, "Well, it was hard to sleep with you and daddy making all that noise all night long."

I wondered what in the world she was talking about. "Sydney, what kind of noise did you hear?"

"All the clanging," she answered. "Were you and daddy banging on pots and pans in my room or in the hall? Were you playing Marching Band?" (Marching Band was a game we played with Sydney where we marched all over the house with her as she played with her toy instruments.)

I froze, stunned. Dan and I absolutely were not banging pots and pans all night long. "Sydney, what did you say?"

She replied, without missing a beat, "It sounded like you and daddy were banging pots and pans in my room."

"We were not banging pots and pans, honey, so I'm not sure what you think you heard. Why do you think that?"

Sydney thought about it, paused, and responded, "Never mind. Now that I think about it, it wasn't pots and pans. It was more like a sword fight. Swords were clanging." She made sword motions she had seen in Peter Pan, her favorite movie as a toddler.

I definitely needed to know what my dad was talking about now. I was so frozen, I couldn't remember his number. Thank goodness for redial. I plunged right in when Dad said, "Hello," much the same as he had done when he called me.

"Dad, what were you saying about spiritual warfare in Sydney's room last night?"

Dad said he was awakened in the middle of the night to pray for

Sydney. In a vision, he saw a demonic creature with a vice grip on her. He began to intercede and fight for her through prayer. He even wielded a sword and fought with the creature until he had cut it off of Sydney. He then heard in his spirit that she had been freed and healed from this oppression.

I was stunned. Sydney had not heard any of that from her pawpaw, and yet she had said she heard swords. I had chill bumps all over me. This was a miracle. Even in my doubt and anger at God, this spoke volumes to me that He was indeed watching over Sydney and He still had plans for her life. I know many of you are shaking your heads in disbelief, especially if your religious upbringing has not taught about spiritual warfare. If I had not lived it and heard that account from my daughter's mouth, I would doubt it, as well.

The proof of deliverance from that oppression and anger was this: After that day Sydney never, ever had another angry outburst at school again! Does she still have Asperger's? Yes. Her brain still processes social situations the same way. She still has anxiety and is totally unsure of what to do in most social situations; but since that intercession, she has never been suspended or expelled again. Remember how I had kept questioning the anger part of her condition, even wondering if it was mental illness? I had questioned if the violence was a spiritual issue. (See Appendix "Asperger's and Anger".) She still had some autism meltdowns when she was overloaded, but she never hit, kicked, spit, destroyed property, ran out of a classroom, or overturned desks at school again.

What I feel happened, and what she confirmed in discussions much later, is that in her experiences at school, her spiritual leaders, teachers, and administrators had let her down, and she was growing bitter and resentful. Satan does not play fair. When a door of anger, bitterness, and unforgiveness opens, even in a child, he will try to step in. I don't believe a child of God can be demon-possessed, but I believe Satan can oppress and inflict mental warfare.

As Sydney continued in therapy during this time, she talked with me about other sounds she heard at night. She swore that she could hear Dan's voice and mine telling her that we did not love her. She said it was like a whispering in her ear, that she would hear us say she was bad, evil, and we did not love her, and we wished she were dead. Never had her father and I said those things, either when she was awake, or when she was asleep. She was suffering, thinking that her life was not important and believing no one wanted her.

She believed her church, her school, and her family didn't want her, so God certainly must not love her, either.

Regarding school, Sydney said once during this time, "I felt like no matter how many good days I had, I would never be able to erase the bad days."

She thought, *The teachers and principals hate me. They can't be trusted. They don't keep their promises, and then they get mad at me when I don't keep my promise.*

She said, "My church school was supposed to always love me. Could I be bad enough that my own family might not want me?"

I had no idea my nine-year-old felt this way. I had no idea she remembered as much as she did. I had no idea that she felt rejected, lied to, betrayed, unloved, and unwanted. This shook her faith in people, church, education, and God. It undermined her confidence in herself, and she felt like no matter if she were perfect, she would never erase those bad days from her ledger. This same day that she shared all of this with me, she said in tears: "Do you think I want to be this way? Do you think I want to hurt people? What's wrong with me?"

How horrible for a third-grade child to suffer so much mentally, emotionally, and spiritually. I was able to convince her that we never, ever whispered those things to her and that we loved her and would do anything to help her.

It was on this day that I had to explain autism/Asperger's. She had heard me tell people she was "autistic," but she thought I was saying "artistic," and she thought that was a good thing. Some parents don't want their child to know their diagnosis. I disagree. (For a detailed explanation on my discussion with Sydney and how to tell your child about their diagnosis, see the Appendix.)

Sydney was flabbergasted that people somehow know how to understand these things that she didn't grasp. I had purchased social skills books and emotional regulation exercise books, and we had incorporated this into the school day. I was doing a social skills lesson with her when she looked at me with her big, blue eyes and said, "Do you remember when your mommy read this book to you, and you learned how to talk to people?"

I was stunned. Not knowing what to say, I stammered, "Well, I don't have autism, so I guess I learned all of this by watching others.

My mom didn't teach me this."

She looked at me incredulously. She couldn't believe that people were born with this ability to decode syntax, tone, and body posture. She shot me a look and bluntly said, "No wonder I didn't understand people and what they meant. Why didn't you tell me a long time ago that I wasn't normal?"

What a discussion sprung into place as we talked about how a person should focus on what they are good at doing, rather than focusing on their challenges. We began a shift of focus, where we concentrated on the concept that autism is only a part of who you are, it does not get to define you. I would say, "You have autism, but it doesn't have to have you." We began to focus on Scripture that talked about who we are in Christ. I had her memorize verses for "Bible class."

We learned: You are fearfully and wonderfully made! And cast your anxiety on Him for He cares for you!

I had an epiphany during this time that there is no exclusion clause for Jeremiah 29:11: "For I know the plans I have for you, plans to prosper you, not to harm you. Plans for a hope and a future." There was no exclusion clause for me or for her; God still had a plan!

It was during this year that my dad gave us all "spiritual names." He said he would call things that aren't as though they were. He would speak new life over us.

Sydney's name was, "Delightful."

Mine, "Joy."

Those names seemed foreign. Sydney, delightful? Me, joyful? It was at least an area of focused prayer and promises to claim for us both.

Sydney begged me not to make her go back to public school. She wanted to be homeschooled the next year. What?

OK, God, you have my attention. I still don't trust You 100 percent, but You have my attention. My study of His character and nature increased. Maybe He did have Sydney's back, but I wasn't certain He had mine. If I was going to homeschool, I needed to hear from God on that myself, because my career as a guidance counselor was going quite well. I loved my students and really enjoyed teaching psychology to high school students. I didn't want to give up my practice and my career to homeschool. I told Sydney I would think about it. She seemed pleased with that answer for the moment.

I felt very encouraged that Sydney was not a human tornado of destruction at school for the rest of third grade. Her teachers said she seemed more peaceful.

"We finally broke that rebellious spirit," they said. But I knew differently.

In mid-May, I began to feel a little nauseous. Could I be pregnant again so soon? Surely, this time God has taken care of this? I mean, He knows that I am on the verge of abandoning my faith, right? The test confirmed I was pregnant.

I thought back to the dream of twins being born in October 2007. That date could still be possible if the babies were born early and not full-term. Sydney had now experienced some form of healing. Maybe the dream could still come to fruition. Now that the school year is about to end and Sydney is less volatile, I shouldn't have as much stress to complicate the pregnancy. I felt my faith being restored. This would be a do-over.

Because I was pregnant and needed to lower my stress levels, I decided that perhaps I should consider homeschooling Sydney. Her dad and I felt that the behavior-focused class was not the place for her to continue, and the school was not considering changing her placement for the next year. We couldn't afford private school. She was expelled from two Christian schools already, so that pretty much would keep her from attending another one. The options seemed bleak. I would resign from my job and at least commit to homeschooling her for fourth grade, until we knew what we would do.

The financial strain of going to one income would be difficult. Our finances were already tight; now it would seem impossible, especially with a baby on the way. As it turned out, the school I worked for wanted a full-time counselor, and I couldn't commit to that. They were concerned about the number of days I had missed due to Sydney's issues, and they were trying to find a way to "let me down gently." After all, my family was the only remaining founding family of this church/school. I took that as confirmation that I was to homeschool.

About this time, I talked with one of our members while we were at a woman's retreat and learned that she was looking to get back into full-time work, as her children were now school age. I suggested she apply for my job. I knew the students would be in capable hands with her, and I had peace to resign.

Chapter Twelve
COUNT IT ALL JOY

Again? Noooooo! God, we had a deal! Miscarriage, now? With me so fragile and my faith flickering? How is this plan Your best for me?

This miscarriage wasn't helping me trust God with every aspect of my life. It wasn't helping me unconditionally love my daughter, either. I felt like I was losing everything. I lost yet another baby, I gave up my career, and I was going to be stuck homeschooling now. I was on God's back burner. I was shelved. I would never be able to use my education and counseling skills. *I just gave up my job for Sydney, God, so it seems to me it was on You to handle this pregnancy.*

I was in a dark place. In my way of thinking, I had no life, no ministry, no career, no use whatsoever! I was stuck in autism hell. It was going to be Asperger's twenty-four/seven.

This is not what I had signed up for, God! Why have me change my major? Why have me even spend the time, energy, and money on a degree I cannot even use? I am not an autism specialist. I do not know how to educate someone with this syndrome! What if I'm not good at it?

This was too much for me to shoulder.

But Dan was pleased that I was homeschooling. He had wanted me to keep Sydney at home all along. He was so happy that he "prayed it into being." Great, God listens to him, I guess. He would frequently share his happiness with the decision. Now, I was mad at him. We were not in a good place in our relationship.

I'm sure Dan thought things were fine. Meanwhile, I would pull into the driveway crying and would have to will myself up to our home. I hated my life. I hated that house. I hated living in the country. I hated that rural county. And I hated that Dan was so happy with all of it! It felt like he had everything he wanted from God, and I had nothing.

My second daughter was my light during this dark time. Erica is one of the happiest children on the planet. She was always there to give me a hug, tell me she loved me, or to smile at me as if I were the most important person on earth. So, when I would have some deep, dark thoughts like running away, I would think, *Erica needs me, and It's selfish to leave a man with two girls to rear.*

This would add to my feeling, though, of being stuck. I felt like I was in the molasses swamp on the Candy Land board. Remember that game? Oh, the dread when you landed in the swamp and had to wait for a certain color card before you could get out and advance. I felt like I was stuck forever, like that card would never come. This emotional swamp was my new home, and I figured I'd better just succumb to it and learn to live there, forever.

I decided to start our 2007-2008 home school year over the summer. I named our home school New Hope Christian Academy. I not only needed hope, I really needed some *new* hope! During the summer, I got a call from our favorite school person, Demonica. It had come to her attention that I had un-enrolled Sydney from school and that I refused to allow her to continue in the behavior-focused class. I explained to her that, as Sydney's parent, I disagreed with the class setting. If that was to be the only option in public school, I had decided that homeschool was a better choice. I was opting out of public school for now.

She said, "Mrs. Holmes, what makes you feel like you are qualified to educate someone like your daughter?"

I thought, *Oh, I don't know. Maybe a BS in psychology, a Master's in counseling, and I'm a licensed professional counselor, and I have subbed and taught every grade from pre-school to twelfth grade. Just pick one, lady!* I refrained from saying any of that out loud.

Calmly, but sarcastically, I said, "You were right all along. She doesn't belong in the school system right now. I believe last school year you mentioned I should homeschool her because she was quite the burden to your teachers. So, look at it now as I have finally agreed to your proposal. I am relieving you of that burden.

"The school also insisted that she remain on the psychotropic drugs, and her father and I want to wean her off of them. So, as we transition to homeschooling, we will work with her doctor to stop the use of medications completely."

Demonica exclaimed, "You cannot take her off her medications. That is neglect! You aren't qualified to homeschool her if you take her off the medications, as well. She needs those medications. Why won't you consider doing the right thing for her and you? You can give up your parental rights, get her into the mental health system, and get her the help she really needs, which you cannot provide."

After a moment of silence in which I needed to compose myself, I coldly responded: "You know, since Sydney is no longer enrolled in public school, your advice is no longer needed or wanted."

Silence on the other end, then click!

Sydney and I both started our home school journey with a bad attitude. Neither of us really wanted to do this. She had this grand dream that homeschooling meant she could get up whenever she wanted and do school in her pajamas with snacks and play time. That was not quite how I imagined it.

Before I could start a fourth-grade curriculum, I had to do some makeup work from third grade. Sydney had missed so many days of school with the acting out and tantrums and suspensions, she had some holes in her education. I'm not blaming her teachers; she missed between twenty to thirty days of academic time each year in in-school suspension, or for other behavior-related reasons.

One night at a prayer service at church, Sydney went up to the altar to pray. It was totally unprompted. She chose a quiet space in the corner. Dan and I wondered what she was praying about.

She came up the aisle and resolutely said she had asked God to forgive her for all the behaviors at school and for "killing her baby brother." She said God told her He was going to heal her.

She said, "I think I need to stop taking my medications because when God heals me I won't need them anymore."

Hmmmm, what to do? We had been reconsidering the medications; yet, I did not want to hinder the faith of a child.

I made an appointment with the psychiatrist. He was totally against removing the medications but agreed to help me wean her, anyway. I figured that because I was homeschooling, I would be the one dealing with any fallout from her coming off the meds. This way,

I would get to deal with her behaviors, unmedicated. She was completely weaned off all medicines that summer and has not been on a psychotropic drug since.

I was slowly coming around spiritually. It felt like God was speaking to me again. I was starting to think that maybe, just maybe, I could trust Him. Maybe He would restore and rebuild. But the battle was uphill. I would start a steady course of trust, then the old thoughts resumed: *Yeah, right! I've heard that before!* As I continued on this cycle of trust and distrust, I heard the Holy Spirit calling me into the ministry.

What? God, I think you have the wrong girl. I'm not even sure I'm on Your side right now. I am not the one. Me, ordained?

I had seen my share of church politics and pastor failings. I had worked at the Christian school and seen how the church and school couldn't seem to work together. *I think I prefer bitterness, resentment, and doing things my way still, thank You. I am not ready to discuss ministry.*

Fourth-grade history was U.S. history. I thought we could combine school with our family vacation and go to Colonial Williamsburg, Yorktown, and Jamestown. The workers at each place dressed and spoke from the time period. There were so many hands-on experiences like the blacksmith shop, the apothecary, the wig shop.

Sydney was in heaven. She was excited about learning. I saw my daughter's eyes light up. I saw her loving to learn again. She remembered everything the actors at the towns said. Her special interest at the time was American Girl Felicity, who was from the American colonial time period, and I was able to tie that into her history lessons. She loved history for the first time.

Not once did she say, "I hate this," or, "I hate you." Once she read the Felicity book series, she became a voracious reader of all the American Girl books. Before, because of how the schools had handled various situations, she had begun to hate reading. Now, I could not keep enough books at the house. We had to visit the library weekly as a field trip to get new books. Her brain was like a sponge; if she read it, she knew it.

Summer school "review" time was very hands-on, field trips, and casual. Fall was coming, and school was on! Erica was in heaven at her school with her BFF cousin, and she was loving every day of it. Sydney and I were home alone to begin the intense, structured, homeschooling schedule. Despite what she might think she wanted, she needed structure. She needed to know what was happening each hour and how the day would flow.

Wondering how God was going to restore my life, my daughter, and my career, I continued on. I just hoped we didn't hate each other at the end of this journey. Right now, it was filled with dread, concern and worry. Oh, and there was no way was I going into the ministry.

I had to turn my house into a school. It really looked more like an institution. We had the daily schoolwork charts, behavior charts, reward charts, and schedules. Every part of the house seemed consumed by charts and school-related materials. There are many different styles of homeschooling, but New Hope Academy was all about structure. When we put up all the charts, Sydney said one important chart was missing to make it like "real school." She wanted a birthday chart.

What do you do with only one student who pretty much knows when her birthday is? She wanted a birthday chart with the birthdays of every extended family member that she knew. Once the house looked like "real school" and she figured out we would have structure and no one would wear pajamas to school, we were on the right track.

At first, she had a meltdown every day, but as we progressed her outbursts became fewer and fewer. Since this was my school, I could incorporate all the things I had hoped a school would have. We worked on anxiety, coping, social stories, social skills, and sensory exercises. Between every core subject and intense time of focus, we took a sensory break.

Sydney was very interested in art, so for socializing I found her an art class that catered to homeschool students. She had a beautiful singing voice and sang constantly, so a homeschool mom at church who was also a music and vocal teacher gave her private singing lessons, and that served as music class. Our church had a lyrical dance group, so that became PE. And her pawpaw took her to horseback riding lessons each week, so she had "specials" that she loved and really looked forward to. The horseback riding became more like hippotherapy for her. She felt free and at peace on the horse she called, "Mandy." As meltdowns and anxiety decreased, schoolwork went quickly. We ended an entire fourth-grade curriculum by Christmas! Then we began fifth-grade work.

Although the homeschool year had begun out of desperation, I learned so much about my daughter that year and about autism. Sydney taught me far more than I taught her.

I learned her anxiety cues. I learned how to help her prevent total meltdowns, to de-escalate. The school's approach had been "escalate her, then teach her to calm down." That approach is mean and cruel. It made Sydney feel violated and betrayed. And the same people who violated her wanted to teach her how to calm down.

But Sydney's thinking went along these lines: *I was doing just fine until you ticked me off, and you need to pay for doing that to me.* She was not thinking, *My teacher is trying to instruct me to de-escalate.*

I learned how she learns best, which environmental cues helped her and which ones detracted and triggered. I learned that anxiety tended to trigger meltdowns and that Sydney's pattern for meltdowns was similar to many persons on the autism spectrum: confusion, frustration, anxiety, meltdown.

I learned about her sensory issues, how to tell when she was feeling more aversive and when she was feeling more seeking, and how to respond to where she was at the moment.

I learned that her sensory issues are real. Despite what the school system had said, sensory issues can detract and impede focus and learning.

I learned how OCD and perfectionism impeded her learning and risk-taking, that she was her own worst enemy. She had a deep feeling of failure that resulted in not trying, which is often misperceived as laziness.

I learned that, sadly, this once-precocious and inquisitive child who loved to learn was terrified of school and teachers. She had learned not to ask questions or she would be called disobedient and disrespectful. She had learned to pretend to understand, so the teachers would leave her alone. She learned not to admit she was confused, or she would be punished. She learned the sad truth that not all teachers are helpful, that some are scary and cannot be trusted.

Her elementary experience had led to resentment, bitterness, and shame. Depression and oppression had entered her life. She couldn't see how God could love her if the adults around her hated her. She felt unwelcome at church, school, and in most people's homes. She could tell people felt afraid or tense around her.

As much as I enjoyed learning about my daughter, I wouldn't be able to keep homeschooling as our finances were dwindling. We only had enough savings to get us through June 1 of the 2007-2008 school year. If something didn't change, I had no idea how we would pay the mortgage. In the midst of the victory we were experiencing with Sydney and my falling in love with her all over again, our financial issues loomed heavy. God was building a new level of trust in me.

Dan and I fasted and prayed about what to do. We began to sense the Lord leading us to a new path, even a new city. Dan considered looking for a new job, and maybe we would even move out of state.

I loved North Carolina. I wanted to grow old and retire there. Maybe we would just move to a different county or school system. Maybe God didn't really mean a whole, new city. Autistic persons don't like change and transition, and anal people like me don't like it, either. As we turned the page on 2007, we entered 2008 with hope that something would be different. Yet there was fear for me because we didn't know what that meant, exactly.

OK, Lord, I remember thinking, *You promised to prosper me and not harm me, right?*

In 2008, the economy started to change nationwide, and the downturn reached the North Carolina markets. Home sales in the rural county where we lived held steady for a little while as people continued to move out of the neighboring metropolitan area to avoid higher taxes. The market wasn't bleak, yet, but it certainly was turning.

Dan worried that his skill set was out of date, and he wouldn't be able to get a job that paid more. This was new territory for us. He had started his current job right out of college, so this was his first real job search. Still, we felt it was our time to move forward. By March, we were ready to start the official job search and prepare the house for sale. Dan and I updated his resume and sent it out.

My aunt in Atlanta, who we had helped with the APC ministry conference, called. We joked about me moving to Atlanta to work as her administrative assistant and continuing to help her with the Atlanta Prophecy Conference. I knew a little about eschatology, but I was by no means a scholar. I had been an administrative assistant before. I realized it wasn't counseling, of course, but perhaps I needed a break from counseling for a while. So, I had part-time work at least, if Atlanta was indeed the place.

And it was. By April, Dan had an interview in Atlanta and was told he could start his new job May 19!

Once the house was on the market, we had a showing every week. I hadn't thought about strangers calling and wanting to see our house, and the strain of keeping it clean and ready to show at a moment's notice. This was an additional level of stress, for Sydney and I were still finishing up the home school year. Because we lived so far out in the county, people would often drive by with their realtor and want to see the house right then because they didn't want to make another trip out to the rural area in which we lived. We would hurriedly pack up and flee the house so it could be shown.

Aspies don't have a super-speed button. They don't move quickly, and they don't like unexpected transitions. To be in the middle of a math lesson and get a call to leave the house for two hours caused distress. Plus, we lived in the middle of nowhere. There was no place to go and hang out.

I had thought that with so many viewings the house would sell in a few months. Well, it didn't, and there certainly was no way it was going to sell by May 19. Dan moved in with my aunt and uncle to start his job in Atlanta, and the girls and I stayed in North Carolina to deal with the house. As the showings continued to increase, it was becoming too stressful for us all to pick up and flee our home at the whim of a potential buyer. Trying to keep a house spotless with children in general is not an easy task, but when one has ASD/OCD and wants things her way and in her order, the stress gets to be too much. In the end, we would have more than fifty first-time viewings and several second and third looks. We would come close to selling three times, only to have the buyers change their minds.

Meanwhile, the sound of the phone ringing would upset Sydney and cause undue panic. "Are we going to have to leave right now?" she would ask. Finally, for stability and peace of mind, the girls and I moved in temporarily with my parents. This would allow the house to be ready at a moment's notice without causing panic in my children. It was quite frustrating to the realtor, I think, because we decided when Dan was able to come home on weekends, we would stay at our house and would not leave. Weekends are typically the time for open houses and viewings, but from five o'clock Friday evening through five o'clock Sunday evening, we would have no viewings, period. We needed family time.

Each Sunday, Dan would head back to Atlanta, and the girls and I would pack up and move back to my parents' home. As summer rolled into fall, I knew the girls would have to be re-enrolled in school. No way was Sydney going back to the school where we were districted—the lock-a-kid-in-the-closet-school. However, the school in my mom's district was the treat-kids-like-criminals school with an ex-cop teacher. I was hoping this would be a miracle moment, that the day before school was to start, the house would sell, we would move to Atlanta, and we would never have to set foot in a that county school ever again.

This was not to be the case.

On occasion, I would head down to Atlanta, and Dan and I would look at schools and houses. We picked out a house in Forsythe County. We picked out a church. It was perfect! We put an offer on a house with the disclaimer that we could only buy if our house sold by August 30, 2008. Well, that was my plan.

It apparently was not God's plan or timing. The school year started, and both girls had to start school in North Carolina. For Sydney, it was back to the place she felt like a failure; yes, and the ex-cop teacher. For Erica, it was a "godless place," as she said, because she had only been to Christian school at this point.

Erica's first day of first-grade public school was hilarious. As I waited in the car line to pick up the girls after school, I saw Erica walking with sheer determination, her arms swinging as she almost ran to the car. Her face showed agitation as she clearly had something on her mind.

The teacher opened the door for her, and the first words out of my first grader's mouth were, "Where have you taken me?" I wasn't sure what she meant. She said: "Mom, they don't pray here! I asked my teacher when she would pray, and she said, 'We don't pray here.' When we went to the library, I asked where the Bible was. She said they don't have a Bible. When it was lunchtime, she didn't pray over the food. This place is godless! I hope you aren't making me come back tomorrow!" And she crossed her arms, satisfied that she had said her piece and certain that her mommy would not make her return to the godless school.

Meanwhile, we were moving to Atlanta, but when? The Aspie ten-year-old was struggling with the back-and-forth of the move and daddy being in and out of town. She has a strong tie to animals, and her dog was being watched by a neighbor. The older dog had come to Mawmaw's with us. She knew she was going back to the school with the ex-cop and, although she did not have any significant behavior issues when she went back to that class, she still felt defeated in that classroom.

The youngest, Erica, with PDDNOS and ADD, was very confused about Daddy being in Atlanta. She thought we were separated or something. She began exhibiting regressive behaviors. She was angry about the upset to her world but wouldn't talk about it. Instead, she began wetting the bed. When Daddy was home and we were at a movie or doing something together, she would soil her clothes. As a counselor, I knew this was her way of telling me she was stressed. The therapy group that had worked with Sydney was available to help Erica through her angst and anger toward Dan and me for the move. Once she was talking it through with her therapist, she was better able to express her stress and worries. The other regressive behaviors subsided.

As the school year dragged on and the housing market downturn finally hit our county, we knew we couldn't keep living in two states much longer. That December, we decided to get an apartment and we'd all live in one state. We had researched where Sydney would attend middle school in Atlanta. However, we could only afford a two-bedroom apartment because we still had a mortgage in North Carolina.

So now the ADD messy, sensory-seeking six-year-old and the uptight, Aspie, OCD ten-year-old would have to share space. Sydney and Erica had never shared a room. It was the longest six months of our lives. Sydney would get up in the middle of the night and move

Erica places to get her out of the room. We would find Erica in the closet, the bathroom, the hall, the living room. Sydney could not stand sharing space with her. I was getting concerned for Erica's mental health and really hoping the North Carolina house would sell soon so we could separate them. The realtor contract expired December 30. Dan had said if the house didn't sell, we would need to rent it. I was not interested in being a landlord two states away; the thought of renting the house was stressful. Please, please, please, Lord, please sell that house!

January 1 came, and we got a call. I thought the deadline had passed, but low and behold, someone made an offer late December 30 and with the thirty-first being a holiday, we were just now getting the news. Thank you, God! Talk about making me sweat it out, but at least we finally had a buyer. We still had to move all of our things then go back to North Carolina to close the deal, but we had one less worry.

I had two heart desires as I prayed about the move to Georgia. I wanted Sydney to find a good best friend, and I wanted her to have a good teacher. A Christian teacher would be amazing. I prayed and prayed: "God, she needs a good teacher and a good friend."

We transferred the kids the last day before Christmas break. I introduced myself to the teacher and noticed she was wearing a cross. I asked if the cross was just a piece of jewelry or if it meant something to her. She said she was a Christian, and she and her husband pastored the church that was literally next door to the school. I gave a brief summary of Sydney and simply said, "If you will get to know her—the real her—she will be a great asset to your class."

Then, I asked for a huge favor. I told her that I really wanted a good friend for Sydney, and if there were a child in the class that was tenderhearted and who could handle kids who were different, I would love to connect them. She said she knew just the girl, and she put Sydney at a desk next to hers. This was a sweet girl from a strong family who not only went to the teacher's church, but who also lived in her neighborhood. The girl and Sydney hit it off, and finally Sydney had a good friend at school.

God had answered the desires of my heart. It made the stress of moving, the apartment life, and the transitions completely worth it. I was full of hope that this move would change things for us. After five years of stress and challenge, maybe, just maybe, relief was in sight.

When we moved, Sydney told me: "I don't want to be the bad kid, anymore, Mom. I want to be the good kid for once."

I replied: "Sydney, you have the ability to start over. Your past is behind you. In fact, this is an opportunity to start over. This is a gift!"

Sydney did struggle with the transition, but she had a clean slate in Georgia. No Demonicas watching after her, no cop-style teachers, no special education separation rooms. She felt free to be herself. And most important to me for starting middle school, she had a friend. Middle school is hard enough, but going it alone would be terrible. And going it alone with Asperger's is a recipe for disaster. Middle school is hard enough for normally developing teens much less when you are "different." (See Appendix for Aspie Teens.)

Actually, Sydney did not seem to be as apprehensive about middle school as I was. I had read many books that talked about the teasing, torment, and bullying Aspie teens face in middle school, and I was concerned about sending my defenseless girl into that fray.

There were some little bumps in the roads, some catty girl issues, but overall middle school was amazing. The teaching staff at the middle school where Sydney was enrolled set the tone for this amazing time for her. When it came time for our first IEP meeting, I had my guard up, ready to fight for my daughter's rights. I was armed with information and the law. But my guard was completely stripped when the teachers at the IEP meeting asked me: "What do you think would best help Sydney to be successful here?"

Was this a trick question? Were they really concerned about what I thought would help Sydney, or was this a trap?

The teachers stared at me, then asked the question again. I wasn't prepared for this. I wasn't prepared for teachers actually to want to see my daughter succeed. Elementary school IEPs had made me a little paranoid. I was prepared for the used car sales approach, where we both say what we want, then dicker over the sticker price. I started to tear up.

The lead teacher was a little taken aback. I gave a brief history of Sydney's elementary years and the struggle it had been to get her help. The teacher sitting on my left was shocked as I spoke of some of the tactics used to get compliance from Sydney.

"Mrs. Holmes," she said. "Let me assure you, that will not happen here. We want to see Sydney succeed. Sydney is very… She's

… What's the word? *Delightful.*"

Delightful? It was mid-fall; by this point in the school year, the teachers were well aware of Sydney's strengths and challenges. They were calling her *delightful?* I had not heard that word used to describe my daughter, ever!

What made Sydney's transition to middle school easier was a co-taught team in a regular education room that had a lead teacher and a special-education teacher. The classroom was not a secluded classroom, and Sydney was doing grade-level work. This class was smaller than the average thirty-five students. There were fewer distractions, fewer sensory issues, and she had more confidence when she wanted to ask a question. No one knew who the special needs kids were, except the two teachers. Sydney felt her teachers cared. She felt that they really did want her to succeed.

In addition to small classrooms, her IEP called for extra time on tests, including standardized tests, and the opportunity to speak with the school counselor if she was struggling socially or academically. There were other things her teachers and I simply agreed on as helps. We opted out of PE the first year of middle school to give Sydney one less locker to deal with in sixth grade. The transition to middle school, of switching to a seven-period day with five or six different teachers, was hard, so we anticipated some stressors or anxieties, and locker time was one of them. Sydney doesn't handle being under time pressure well, and she already had hand-eye coordination issues, so getting into a locker quickly, getting what she needed, and heading to class was difficult to do in a four-minute period. I requested that her locker be close to her homeroom, near a bathroom, and a top locker, if at all possible.

Sydney's teachers told her in private that if she struggled, they would help her and not count her tardy if she was slightly late due to locker issues. This lifted a huge anxiety from her. When Sydney got her schedule, her caseworker would arrange for us to come to school a day or so early for her to practice finding her classes and walking out the schedule.

Sydney wanted to be a part of band, but she didn't want a reed instrument or something that would touch her mouth. The band teacher, who was well aware of Asperger's, let Sydney try out for percussion, and she was able to participate with percussion instruments.

We put a plan in place for days when the normal class schedule was altered: picture day, assemblies, field days, and special speakers. This plan would prompt Sydney and help ease her anxiety. Best of all, her teachers wanted her to succeed and were open to my suggestions. They were interested in preventing meltdowns, and they understood the embarrassment of such an event in middle school.

For the first time, Sydney started and finished a school year at the same school! In fact, she finished all three years of middle school at the same school. In sixth grade, she received the "Climate Award," which is given to a student who has exhibited exemplary behavior. She didn't get in any form of trouble or discipline her entire sixth-grade year. By eighth grade, she wanted to try the gifted classes she had tested into a year previously, but this meant giving up the support of the two-teacher team. She also wanted to try a world language, which had previously been an issue. Had we finally turned a corner? Sydney still had Asperger's Syndrome; she still had anxiety. But she had learned some self-control. She had learned coping skills for some of her sensory issues.

More than once in her three years of middle school, the teacher said she was delightful, which brought me great joy. Sydney now was known amongst her student body as a "goody two-shoes." I asked her if that bothered her.

"No," she said, "I know what I am capable of, and "goody two-shoes" is better than being the bad kid."

I believe the key ingredient in Sydney's successful transition from elementary school to middle school was a mental shift in her attitude and spirit. She'd had years of being told she was trouble, challenging, and problematic. She was told she would never be allowed in a mainstream classroom again and that she would fail. And she expected to fail. She did not have hope. Aspies are already very hard on themselves, often demanding perfection when perfection is not possible. They tend to beat themselves mentally for mistakes and expect that because of their academic intelligence and skill, they should excel in every area of their lives.

In the summer before our move, Sydney began to feel more empowered about her situation, and she developed a resolve that if given another chance, she would do things differently in school. Her motivation changed, and her opinion about herself and her abilities shifted.

The early diagnosis was crucial in our story, so that Asperger's/ASD was something we could work on and talk about as a family, so that by adolescence, Sydney had a better understanding of what it meant to have Asperger's as a syndrome. As I told her many times, she knew that Asperger's does not define her as a person. And to this day, I have *never* received another behavior call from any of her teachers.

As a high school student, Sydney takes the lead in whether to discuss her Asperger's with outsiders. She has told some people she trusts what her struggles can be. As she has continued into high school, the IEP team has still been a pleasure to work with. I don't have one negative word about the administrators and special education team at the schools we have attended in Georgia. For all the stress and trauma of the transition, the move to Atlanta was well worth it. A clean slate made all the difference for Sydney. Her problems didn't magically disappear when we moved to Atlanta, but I never got another call from a teacher about her behavior.

In Atlanta, she has been in the gifted and honors program and even taken AP classes. At the printing of this book, she is entering her senior year of high school, is also enrolled in community college, and has a 3.8 GPA. She has even been accepted into the top two colleges of her choice. On Diagnosis Day, all of these things had been written off.

Sydney has had so many accomplishments. She has her driver's license, and, during the summer of 2015, she had a part-time job as a junior camp counselor to help pay for her car. She has lettered in cross-country and marching band, and participated in Fellowship of Christian Athletes. She has played both percussion and saxophone in the performance band, runs track, jumps hurdles, and is co-consul of the Latin club.

She is a model student. But what I am most proud of is her ability to be a friend to anyone of any race, creed, disability, orientation, or religion. Everyone who knows her knows of her faith, and although she is strong in her faith, she is not a bully, nor is she demeaning to those with different beliefs. High school has presented challenges with bullies and mean girls and broken friendships and promises, but I have watched Sydney blossom in her faith, forgiveness, and spiritual maturity. I, too, have had to grow in my faith, forgiving those who have hurt her along the way.

Is life a bed a roses now? Is everything a walk in the park? Not at all. The years 2008 through 2011 were bliss compared to previous years. But the previous difficulties grew my faith to get me through the set of trials that came in 2012 to 2014. That has been God's record in my life. He uses trials as building blocks to grow my faith, so I can move from one set of trials to another. The years 2012 to 2014 are a story that doesn't involve autism, but cancer, surgeries, health crises, financial crises, and too much of my personal health to dive into in this book.

How has God worked all of this to my good? Isn't that the question I started with? I consult with families all over the nation. I am able to reach out to families who are at the beginning of their journey and offer them hope. Hope is powerful. I speak on marriage and family life with a child on the spectrum at various conferences for the American Association of Christian Counselors. Sydney blogs and writes about her journey, and that helps other teens on the spectrum find their voice.

This is not a journey I would have chosen, but now I can see that God has worked all things out for my good. He did have plans to prosper me and not to harm me. In this life we will have troubles, but He gives us peace that He walks each step with us, and if we let Him He will restore what the locusts have stolen, and He will bring beauty from ashes. I don't think I was chosen to raise an ASD child. I don't think Sydney and Erica were smitten with ASD as a curse or punishment. However, God knew autism would be in my future, and He prepared me for it every step of the way. I am the one who fought Him and doubted Him. Yet, He was faithful. He continued to make my path straight and to order my steps.

In 2010, I was attending my first American Association of Christian Counselors conference since Sydney's Diagnosis Day. I was unable to travel and attend conferences after Diagnosis Day. At this conference, a speaker was presenting his seminar and mid-sentence he said, "I don't know why I am saying this now, but we are told to count it all joy."

At that moment, the Holy Spirit spoke to me. I was so overcome that I began to sob. I had to excuse myself. I felt the Lord say that I had indeed grown in faith and had restored my trust in Him, but I had never regained my joy. It was time for me to count it all joy, to realize that the gift He gave me—yes, the child with autism—was a perfect gift and that gift would be used to complete my calling in ministry and counseling. I felt Him telling me that He alone would open up doors for me to minister and to speak to families who would walk a similar journey. My personal story combined with my counseling training and ministry would be the fullness of the mantle He had placed on me. Since 2011, He has allowed me to be a speaker for the American Association of Christian Counselors where I speak on special needs families and issues concerning autism spectrum disorder.

Autism opened my eyes to the fact that for most of my life, my faith has been more in my own abilities and goals than in God's power and His plans for me. But when I put my issues into God's hands, He worked them out for my good. My joy has been restored.

ADDITIONAL PAGES

These last pages are intended as a resource for families with autistic members, particularly children. Starting on this page is a review of the Treatments and Protocol that we applied to Sydney and some discussion of how those worked for her. Following the Treatments and Protocol is the Appendix, which includes various articles I have written for academic journals or blogs on the subject of autism and Asperger's Syndrome. I hope you will find these helpful.

Autism Treatments and Protocol

Counselor

Very early on, after Sydney's expulsion from first-grade Christian school, the first thing we felt she needed was a counselor. As people began to reject her and she began to realize she was different, I felt as a counselor myself that she needed someone to talk to about these feelings. As she got older, these sessions morphed into helping her deal with anxiety and frustration. She trusted her therapist and looked forward to having her "talking time." I learned later that Dr. Tony Attwood advocates cognitive-behavior therapy (CBT) for children and adolescents with Asperger's, particularly during the adolescent years when anxiety and depression can be so problematic. We wanted a therapist who would reinforce our belief system, so we chose a Christian counselor.

The therapist was primarily for Sydney, but she was helpful to my husband and me, as well. Sometimes, we needed support, and I certainly needed someone to vent to as I educated myself on autism and Asperger's. I felt so frustrated as I tried to help Sydney at home, but I mainly needed this kind of support when I was advocating at school.

Occupational Therapist (OT)

Occupational therapists help ASD children deal with sensory issues. Sensory issues are a major reason ASD children aren't able to focus in the classroom. The year Sydney's class was in a learning cottage (trailer) she had difficulty with the noise level in the classroom. Thirty kids in such a small place was challenging. Add to that the sound of lawn mowers nearby, or cars, or children playing outside during recess—all of these were distractions Sydney had problems overcoming.

Sometimes, just the noise from the heating or AC system or the feel of the heat or AC could trigger problems. Other things—like the feel of her clothes, the sounds other students make, the ticking of a clock, or the close proximity of desks—become sensory issues that can cause a meltdown in the ASD class. I had to educate myself on sensory processing issues and their interaction with ASD and how they affected Sydney at home, school, church, and the community. This is why an OT is such a good resource. There is now a plethora of books on the market about sensory processing disorders and sensory integration issues. One of my favorite authors is Carol Stock Kranowitz.

Physical Therapy (PT)

In our ASD education process, we learned that motor skills tend to be delayed for the ASD child. They get frustrated because, although they may have the focus to do a task, their bodies work against them actually completing the task. For some kids, it may be fine motor skills, which are required to tie shoes, button shirts, or grasp a pencil. For others, it's the gross motor skills needed to run, jump, and skip. For some ASD kids, it is both. According to our physical therapist (PT), Sydney's gross motor skills were about a year behind, and her fine motor skills nearly two years.

She always struggled with tying her shoes and getting the proper hold on her pencil grip. It was also hard for her to jump and land on both feet. Sometimes, it was difficult not to simply assume that she would grow out of these things, or to figure that she just was not graced athletically. But to her, particularly because she was academically smart, it was very frustrating.

We originally started doing PT, but when we realized that the insurance company lumped OT and PT in the same therapy restriction, therefore, giving us a combined total of only thirty sessions a year, we decided to see what other options existed for building motor skills. About that time, a Christian karate group did a presentation at the school where I was working, and I decided to call them. I knew that martial arts teach focus and balance and improves mind and body cooperation. We went for a trial class, then decided this would be her PT replacement. Sydney went to karate two to three times a week for much less than PT would have cost us.

The instructor was very patient with Sydney's Asperger issues, including her running out of the karate dojo or refusing to do something on the first request. Sydney was very successful with this program. She reached the level just one belt from junior black belt. We stopped because the last level of belt would require some weapons training, and with her emotional instability at times, I was not comfortable with her learning how to wield a knife. But for those few years we were there, it was a great asset to her. It helped with focus, balance, following instructions, motor skills and self-confidence. Individual sports tend to work best for ASD kids. Sports such as swimming, tennis, and martial arts that are not group-based can help an ASD child achieve on many levels.

Diet and Chelating

Further into our ASD education, we began to hear about natural alternatives for helping reverse symptoms of ASD through diet and chelating. Chelating is a process to remove toxins and heavy metals from the body. It is not the scope of this book to discuss leaky gut and the brain and gut interaction; there are plenty of resources on that. We decided to contact a Defeat Autism Now (DAN) doctor and to get educated on diet and chelation. Let me be very clear: If you decide to use chelation, you can only do so under the care of an MD or DO (Doctor of Osteopathic Medicine) who is certified to prescribe it. There are many over-the-counter options, but there are some risks involved in chelation and understanding that risk is paramount.

Chelation works by drawing out the impurities through the kidney and liver, and it is of utmost importance to follow the protocol and have liver and kidney blood tests done. In fact, we stopped the chelation when Sydney's liver numbers weren't looking quite right. The chelation is expensive because the doctors who can help you, like DAN doctors, are rarely covered by insurance; hence, you pay for the medical visits and check-ups completely out of pocket. The chelating medications or drops are also not currently covered by insurance since it is not FDA-approved. Furthermore, you have to be careful what vitamins and minerals you give your child during the process, and the cost of those supplements is very high. This process **must** be done under medical supervision.

In addition to this protocol, the DAN doctor suggested we go completely gluten and casein (dairy) free—sometimes, this is called the GFCF diet. We were already using the Feingold diet, which is an organic diet free of dyes, artificial flavors, chemicals, and preservatives. Their food was 100 percent organic; the GFCF made it very expensive, and trying to stick to the plan at school was extremely tough, particularly with birthday parties and school parties popping up every other week. Add to that the fact that many ASD kids tend to have environmental and food allergies, and the menu of foods my daughter could eat was very limited. But we felt we had some success with this. To this day, I can tell by behavior when one of my children has been eating too much of something with gluten or artificial colors.

Intelligence Testing

We also did some additional intelligence-type testing to see where exactly Sydney's challenges and skill sets were. It's important to know from the education standpoint what areas might be weak and how to build those weak areas without frustrating the child. They are already off developmentally with motor skills and sensory issues, having to eat strange foods and, in Sydney's case, having a twenty-two-pill vitamin supplement routine. The protocols are not easy and not cheap. And not to forget the part about the laboratory testing of hair, feces, urine, and blood that is done to determine what heavy metals and toxins may be causing the issues and, hence, the decision on which supplements and vitamins need to be added. Any kind of testing involving needles and bodily fluids with an ASD child is not for the faint of heart.

APPENDICES

Appendices Contents

APPENDIX I

Light It Up Blue:
Understanding Autism Spectrum Disorders
Dr. Eric Scalise and Stephanie C. Holmes, MA BCCC

What do music composers Amadeus Mozart and Ludwig Van Beethoven, artists Michelangelo and Vincent Van Gogh, physicists Sir Isaac Newton and Albert Einstein, Renaissance polymath Leonard Da Vinci, President Thomas Jefferson, and Microsoft founder Bill Gates have in common? All are known or suspected of fitting somewhere on the autism spectrum. As a "spectrum disorder," autism represents a wide array of symptoms—from mild to severe—that affect individuals differently. However, a common core of indicators is at play, influencing the neurological development of social skills, empathy, communication, and flexible behavior. This developmental disability crosses every social, racial, ethnic, and socioeconomic group.

Autism is a label feared by parents, a challenge for educators, a subject of movies and books, an often-misunderstood disorder, and is sometimes caught up in a swirl of emotional controversy. So, what drives the need for greater recognition? And has autism reached epidemic proportions? According to research conducted by the Centers for Disease Control (CDC), an estimated one out of eighty-eight children has been identified with autism spectrum disorder (ASD), with boys (one in fifty-four) about five times more likely to be diagnosed than girls (one in 252). [1] April 2 of every year is known as World Autism and Awareness Day, and Light it up BLUE is a global initiative that was created to get the message out.

Dr. James Coplan, a neurodevelopment pediatrician from the University of Pennsylvania School of Medicine, maintains that the increase is primarily due to changes in diagnostic criteria. He states that the way current statistics are reviewed is directly related to the number of children who receive services under the heading of ASD. Prior to 1975, there were few, if any, educational rights for "handicapped" children, so no definitive baseline exists. However, Dr. Martha Herbert, a pediatric neurologist at Harvard Research

School of Medicine, believes otherwise. Her team examined the rise of rates as a function of the change in diagnostic criteria from the Diagnostic and Statistical Manual of Mental Disorders-III (DSM-III) to the DSM-IV. Yet, broadening of the criteria still accounts for only 400 percent of the 1200 percent increase from the 1980s, leaving a staggering escalation of 800 percent in the last 25 years not attributable to changes in the diagnostic benchmarks.

Much of the debate centers on incidence versus prevalence rates. Incidence refers to the number of new cases that emerge in the birthrate of a population. Prevalence is the percentage of a population affected by a disease or disorder. To qualify ASD as an epidemic, the incidence based on birthrate must be determined, and this is not known with absolute certainty. Nevertheless, research has clearly shown a significantly higher prevalence of ASD among the present generation, indicating an "explosion" of ASD diagnoses, but not necessarily an epidemic.

Signs and Symptoms

Symptoms of ASD vary from person to person, generally falling into three categories: social impairment, communication difficulties, and repetitive/stereotyped behaviors. [Added in 2015, the DSM-5 combined these three categories into two. See Stephanie's article, "Did the DSM-5 Get It Right on ASD?"] They manifest in a child's early developmental period and impair social, occupational, or other areas of functioning. The DSM-5 criteria include the following (severity is specified according to the need for support)[2]:

1. Deficits in social communication and social interaction across multiple contexts.
    - In social-emotional reciprocity, ranging from an abnormal social approach to a reduced sharing of interests, emotions, or affect; to the failure to initiate or respond to social interactions.
    - In nonverbal communication, behaviors used for social interaction, ranging from poorly integrated verbal-nonverbal communication; to abnormalities in eye contact and body language; to total lack of facial expressions and nonverbals.
    - In developing, maintaining, and understanding

relationships, ranging from difficulties in adjusting behaviors to fit various social contexts; to difficulties in sharing imaginative play or in making friends; to the absence of interests in peers.

2. Restricted and repetitive patterns of behavior, interests, or activities.

- Stereotypical or repetitive motor movements, use of objects or speech (for example, lining up toys, echolalia, or saying idiosyncratic phrases).

- Insistence on sameness, inflexible adherence to routines or ritualized patterns of verbal/nonverbal behavior (for example, extreme distress at small changes, difficulties with transitions, rigid thinking patterns, greetings, rituals).

- Highly restricted, fixated interests that are abnormal in focus of intensity.

- Hyper- or hypo-reactivity to sensory input or an unusual interest in sensory aspects of the environment (for example, apparent indifferences to pain/temperature, adverse responses to specific sounds or textures, excessive smelling/touching of objects, visual fascination with lights or movements).

In the DSM-IV, Asperger's Syndrome (named after pediatrician Hans Asperger) was added to the category of Pervasive Development Disorders and referred to as part of the autism spectrum. Since that time, Asperger's has become a common term in the fields of medicine, psychology, and education. A controversial change in the DSM-5 is the removal of the term Asperger's Syndrome as a distinct disorder. The DSM-5 revision team decided the term *autism* was too broad and hence, was responsible for the increase in autism diagnoses over the past twenty years. The main debate centered on whether "Kanner" or "classical autism" (named after child psychiatrist Leo Kanner) is clinically significant from Asperger's. In the DSM-IV and DSM-IV-TR, autism included classic autism; Asperger's Syndrome; childhood disintegrative disorder; Rhett's Syndrome; Tourette's Syndrome; and pervasive developmental disorder, not otherwise specified (PDDNOS); as well as atypical autism.

The Yale School of Medicine analyzed people currently diagnosed with DSM-IV criteria and then applied the new DSM-5 standard on the sample.[3] The updated criteria resulted in 75 percent of the sample retaining the diagnosis. The majority of the remaining 25 percent were those previously diagnosed with PDDNOS or Asperger's Syndrome. One major concern for treatment professionals, as well as parents of the diagnosed child, is that those considered to be "higher-functioning" may be excluded from the diagnosis and, therefore, much needed services within the educational system.

Dr. Tony Attwood, a world-renowned autism expert, argues that even though the DSM-5 may exclude Asperger's Syndrome, the ICD-9/ICD-10 medical classification system used by the World Health Organization retained the terminology and distinction. According to Attwood, those with Asperger's (sometimes called Aspies) are usually not diagnosed until between the ages of eight and eleven and perhaps even later for girls (ages ten to thirteen). The problem lies with the new DSM-5 criteria where clinical impairment must be noted before the child turns three. Unfortunately, associated symptoms may not be recognized until the child is school age and struggling with psychosocial skill development among peers. Advocates for Asperger's as a separate disorder must wait to see what the impact will be on future diagnoses, treatment interventions, and resource availability.

Since Asperger's is a relatively recent term, many went through childhood, adolescence, and early adulthood undiagnosed, especially women who blend into mainstream culture better. More adults are being diagnosed in their late twenties and thirties today, usually after a child or close family member is diagnosed. Asperger's also affects marriage because Aspies grapple with reciprocal conversation and difficulty showing empathy and outward expressions of love. Studies show 80 percent of marriages with an Aspie partner end in divorce. There is scant information available on counseling Aspie couples, but traditional marriage counseling tends to be unsuccessful, and non-ASD spouses need to be better educated.

Etiological Factors

The exact causes of ASD are not fully understood or universally agreed upon. Possible triggers include genetic/chromosomal abnormalities or syndromes (see generationally), severe infections that impact the brain (for example, meningitis, encephalitis, celiac disease), metabolic or neurological factors, and exposures to certain toxins or illness during pregnancy (e.g., rubella, some chemicals). Additional considerations include certain prescription drugs taken during pregnancy, such as valproic acid (brand name Depakote, a mood stabilizing drug used to treat epilepsy and migraines), maternal gestational diabetes, bleeding after the first trimester, and premature and/or low birth weight in children. Neuroanatomical studies point to a possible link regarding a combination of brain enlargement in some areas of the brain and reduction in others during prenatal and postnatal development. Other studies are beginning to explore the potential connection between ASD and certain co-morbid conditions in a person's peripheral nervous, immune, and gastrointestinal systems.

There are many (added after print—in the medical field, as well as parents) who believe childhood vaccinations especially the MMR (measles-mumps-rubella) vaccine is a primary contributor to ASD. Some point to the age and scheduling of various vaccines given to a child at one time. This particular controversy was based on a 1998 article by British physician Andrew Wakefield. The study was partially retracted in 2004, fully retracted in 2010, and Dr. Wakefield was stripped of his medical license for unethical conduct related in research. Following the initial claims of Dr. Wakefield, several large epidemiological studies were commissioned by the CDC, the American Academy of Pediatrics, the Institute of Medicine, and the U.S. National Academy of Sciences, all of which failed to corroborate the original findings. Nevertheless, some individuals continue to inquire whether certain vaccines can "activate" genetic triggers already present, thereby resulting in the development of ASD.

Assessment and Diagnosis

Assessing and diagnosing ASD is complex and time-consuming. It can be several years after signs and symptoms first appear before an official diagnosis is given. This tendency may have something to do with the lack of awareness on the part of the parents, understandable caution over misdiagnosing a child's condition, or concerns regarding a potentially damaging "label." Screening for ASD is usually comprehensive as there is no single medical test to confirm a diagnosis. Multiple evaluations by healthcare professionals who specialize in developmental disorders are usually necessary (e.g., child psychologists, child psychiatrists, speech pathologists, audiologists, developmental pediatricians, pediatric neurologists, special education teachers). Diagnosis assessments typically include a parental interview; a medical exam, which may incorporate neurological and genetic testing; a hearing test to rule out audiological problems; and a screening for lead poisoning because of its ability to mimic autism-like symptoms. Other evaluative measures may comprise of speech and language assessments, cognitive testing, and adaptive functioning (e.g., the ability to problem solve and demonstrate appropriate social, verbal, and nonverbal skills), and sensory-motor assessment.

Interventions and Treatment Protocols

There are various opinions about "curing" or "reversing symptoms" of ASD. Most researchers understand ASD as a lifelong pervasive development disorder and, therefore, it is not usually discussed in terms of a cure. However, early diagnosis and treatment consistently utilizing a broad range of tailored interventions are believed to be the key. With standard protocols, it is often imperative to have medical supervision (an experienced M.D. or Dr. of Osteopathic Medicine) due to related health risks.

- Education Services: By law, schools are not required to provide assistance absent a current (within three years), formal diagnosis. Once a diagnosis is established, a meeting for special services can be scheduled at the child's school, which then makes him or her eligible for services under the Individuals with Disabilities Education Act (IDEA). Parents need to brace themselves for what may be a tumultuous journey, especially when the student is on the higher-functioning end of the spectrum. Many states have an Autism Society or Autism Advocacy groups who understand state/federal laws regarding special services and can help parents navigate the system.
- An Individualized Educational Plan (IEP) is developed, based on test scores, teacher observations, and professional recommendations. Resources available to children can include small group settings to take tests/quizzes, extra time to

complete assignments, occupational/speech therapy, social skills training, guidance/counseling for anxiety and transitions and in some cases, one-to-one staff support for children who can do the mainstream work but require behavior assistance. School files typically will not follow into adult life because a diagnostic label for the purpose of educational intervention ends with the twelfth grade. However, the correct diagnosis can make a world of difference in resources and tools for the student from grades K-12.

- Occupational Therapy: Finding an occupational therapist (OT) outside the school setting who understands and works with ASD and sensory processing disorder (SPD) is important. Many children struggle with fine motor skills (e.g., holding a pencil, tying shoes, working a zipper), daily living skills, personal space issues, sensory issues, and self-injury. An OT will evaluate and help determine a tailored plan of action.

- Physical Therapy: ASD children also struggle with gross motor skills (e.g., sitting in a chair, walking gait, skipping, running, standing without falling over). Many students have underdeveloped muscle groups that could be strengthened with physical therapy (PT). Available PT options include dance and movement, gymnastic type skill building, aquatic therapy, hippotherapy (uses the characteristic movements of a horse to provide sensory-motor input), martial arts, and various types of play therapy. A good PT evaluation can help the parents make choices for their children's muscle tone and muscle group development.

- Applied Behavioral Analysis (ABA): ABA (a form of behavior modification that excludes hypothetical constructs) can foster basic skills such as looking, listening, and imitating, as well as complex skills such as reading, conversing, and understanding another person's perspective. It can involve additional cost, but has been clinically shown to improve the behavioral aspects of ASD children.

- Social Skills Training: Many children do not grasp social context (e.g., how to read people's body posture or tone, initiate or maintain conversations, initiate play/friendships, or recognize bullying or mean behavior toward them). This is more related to social IQ or etiquette, and there are tools parents can incorporate in conjunction with a therapist. Pivotal Response Training for self-management and Developmental, Individual Differences, Relationship-based Approach (DIR, also called "Floor Time") TM are two examples.

- Cognitive-Behavioral Therapy (CBT): ASD is not a mental disease or disorder, yet is often co-morbid with attention deficit disorder, obsessive-compulsive disorder, anxiety disorders, hoarding, emotional dysregulation and other behavioral issues. Children will eventually realize they are different from their peers and may need help processing these differences. Individuals often struggle with anxiety and depression (normal markers may be masked) and the upward trend of ASD teen suicide has become alarming (60 percent contemplate suicide by age thirteen). Having a competent therapist is a valuable asset to families as they navigate educational milestones and new challenges awaiting each transition.

- Medical Supervision: Many in the mainstream medical community believe autism is primarily genetic and structural deficits, thereby emphasizing a combination of behavioral therapies and pharmaceutical treatments. Other professionals, however, strongly believe ASD results from more biological factors (toxins, immune deficiencies, gastrointestinal inflammation). The Defeat Autism Now (DAN!) project, created by the Autism Research Institute outlined an approach to treatment called the "DAN! Protocol," based on biomedical theory. Here, doctors often recommend chelation (removing heavy metals from the body—especially lead, mercury, and arsenic), vitamins and supplements, a gluten/casein-free (GFCF) diet, and various options of detoxing before considering a biomedical treatment.

While ASD remains a complex issue requiring ongoing research, a proactive approach with children and their families is important— letting them know that different does not mean less than or defective. The promise of Jeremiah 29:11 is inclusive for all those with ASD: "'For I know the plans I have for you,' declares the Lord, 'plans to prosper you and not harm you, plans to give you hope and a future.'"

Authors:

- Eric Scalise, PH.D, is the former vice president of the American Association of Christian Counselors. He is a Licensed Professional Counselor, a Licensed Marriage and Family Therapist, the former Department Chair for the Counseling Program at Regent University in Virginia Beach, Virginia. He has more than thirty-two years of clinical and professional experience in the mental health field. Eric is an author, a national and international conference speaker, and frequently consults with organizations, clinicians, ministry leaders, and churches on a variety of issues.

- Stephanie C. Holmes, MA, is a Certified Autism Specialist, a Credentialed Christian Counselor with the Georgia Board of Examiners for Christian Counselors and Therapists, a Board Certified Christian Counselor with the International Board of Christian Counselors and was formerly a Licensed Professional Counselor in North Carolina. When Stephanie's oldest daughter was diagnosed Asperger's Syndrome, she changed her focus to the world of educational plans and understanding how to help special needs' students in the classroom and their families. A current focus includes counseling and consultation for couples with a high-functioning autism partner. She practices at her home church, Calvary Church Atlanta.

END NOTES:

1. Centers for Disease Control Prevention. Retrieved from cdc.gov/ncbdd/autism/data.html.
2. American Psychiatric Association (2013). Diagnostic and Statistical Manual of Mental Disorders (5th ed.). Washington, DC: American Psychiatric Publishing, p. 50-59.
3. McPartland, C.; Reichow, B. & Volkmar F.R. (2012) Sensitivity and Specificity of Proposed DSM-5 Diagnostic Criteria for Autism Spectrum Disorder. Journal of American Academy of Child and Adolescent Psychiatry, 51, 368-383.

Reprinted from Christian Counseling Today *Vol. 20, No. 2, Childhood Development Disorders. With permission from the American Association of Christian Counselors.*

APPENDIX II

ASD/Asperger's and Empathy: Everyone Can Do Some, Some Can Do More, and a Few Can Do Much

It is a common myth that people with ASD/Asperger's lack empathy. While it is true that persons on the spectrum struggle with social interactions, have mind-blindness, and struggle with appropriate display of empathy at times, it is simply not true that they lack empathy. The truth is, they simply do empathy differently. In fact, studies are showing that people on the spectrum tend to have over-active empathy.

My lead pastor, Brian Campbell of Calvary Church Atlanta, has a heart for missions. If he has said the above quote once, he has said it a hundred times, "Everyone can do some, some can do more, and a few can do much." How I have recently seen this phrase play out in my fifteen-year-old daughter with Asperger's Syndrome (autism spectrum disorder) has blessed me beyond measure. You can read about my personal journey of faith when my daughter was diagnosed with autism, how it rocked my world, shattered my faith, then grew my faith on the American Association of Christian Counselor's blog at aacc.net. Autism is not really dealt with much in the Christian community. If you try to search for help from a Christian perspective, there is little out there. When my daughter received her diagnosis in 2004, my life changed. See, I was a professional Christian counselor and was growing my practice and ministry when the diagnosis turned life upside down. Nothing made sense. *God, what are you doing? How can you let this happen to me? How can you let this happen to her?* For several years, life was a blur and dominated by autism. I thought my life and ministry were over. What could I possibly do to help people now? How could God use me? What would her life be like? What could she contribute to this world?

A few years ago speaker Jennifer Pasquale came to our church and talked about child sponsorship, specifically with Latin America ChildCare (LACC) in Costa Rica. Our family began to sponsor a child. Soon, each of us would have a child to write to and encourage in sponsorship. As a family we prayed for these children. We were sending money, praying for them, and writing to them. We were doing SOME. Last year, my daughter Sydney (with ASD) had to choose a project for her Gold Award (the highest honor in Girl Scouts) and the answer lay in the *Pentecostal Evangel* article by Mary Mahon about LACC and "Chicas de Promesa." That was it! Sydney's project was to help Mary with Chicas de Promesa. This would require MUCH from a then fourteen- now fifteen-year-old girl with autism.

Sydney has great anxiety when it comes to public speaking, but this project would require a lot of standing before audiences. She had to get in front of the Girl Scout Council and request items to be donated for "Chicas de Promesa." She also made a Power Point presentation to request funds from ministries to help get her to Costa Rica. She babysat, dog-walked, baked, sold things, and worked very, very hard to raise money for the items needed for the clubhouse. She worked with local author Lorraine Fast to be trained in the area of Human Trafficking/Sexual abuse and to get seminar materials to teach to the girls in San Jose, Costa Rica. She had a translation team translate the materials into Spanish.

What? She's not supposed to do all that. She has autism! But she spent a week in San Jose, Costa Rica, working with four schools in the LACC system, and she used money donated to purchase items for the clubhouse in Linde Vista that was mentioned in the *Pentecostal Evangel* article.

The highlight of the trip was meeting the child our family sponsors in Linde Vista and seeing what monthly sponsorship does for children. I had a lot of time to reflect on this trip, and I had to smile as I watched my daughter work with the team at LACC and saw the faces of the girls that she was reaching out to about a big topic such as human trafficking prevention. There were naysayers that told me to have Sydney committed, that she could never possibly interact with people or contribute anything to this world. As a mom, I just needed to "accept that she would never have a fulfilling life." My family and I chose to ignore that and to speak life over her. Her journey has been hard, but I have seen miracle after miracle and watched God use this wonderful creation for His glory and His purpose. Does she still have Asperger's? Yes, but she has had significant improvement over the past six to seven years. A child who was expelled from school (grades kindergarten through third grade) for "behavior" issues spoke life into the girls of San Jose, Costa Rica.

Seven years ago, I never could have imagined this day when my daughter, who struggles so much with anxiety and public speaking, would be reaching out and ministering through the platform of her Gold Award in Girl Scouts. I thank God that He did not give up on me and that He never gave up on Sydney's life. What the world sometimes says is useless or not important, God can use for His glory. He truly gives "beauty for ashes" and "joy for mourning."

In 2012, Sydney received the Miriam Award (highest award through the Assemblies of God's Girls Ministries) for "strong faith despite a disability" and was given this award when she graduated the Friends program (sixth grade through eighth grade) at a Georgia District Celebration. Sydney's story of faith so moved our Children's Ministry Director for Georgia, Gay Wall, that he put Sydney's story on the Georgia website.

As I say often when I speak, there is no exclusion clause in Jeremiah 29:11. God can use *everyone*! So, what is holding you back? What excuses do you use for why God cannot use you? We all can pray, send money and contributions, and invite missionaries to our churches, but what can *you* do? My autistic daughter showed me the meaning of my pastor's phrase "Everyone can do some, some can do more, a few can do much." Which one are you?

APPENDIX III

Supporting Families with an Asperger's/ASD Child: How Can You Help?

Stephanie C. Holmes, MA, BCCC, Certified Autism Specialist

As I was driving my oldest daughter to high school recently, I briefly reflected on her tumultuous elementary school years. I was a slave to my cell phone, looking every five minutes to see if the school would be calling me to come pick up my daughter—*again*! Those were tough years. I thought back to the day of her first expulsion from kindergarten and the sinking feeling that this behavior I was seeing could be "that thing" I learned about in graduate school— Asperger's Syndrome.

Even though I held a graduate degree in counseling and an undergraduate degree in psychology, knowledge of the symptoms of a disorder does nothing to help you live with a lifelong developmental disorder in your child. The thought was terrifying to me. The school system referred me to the TEACCH Autism Program, a program available to parents in North Carolina. TEACCH was instrumental in diagnosing not only my oldest daughter with Asperger's and mild OCD, but, later, my youngest daughter with PDDNOS and mild ADHD.

TEACCH was a wealth of information to me when I was overwhelmed and trying to educate myself on what to do to help my children. One of the biggest things TEACCH did was give me permission to reach out for support. I'm an independent soul who tries to conquer the world on my own and asking for help is not in my repertoire of tools for coping.

I was told to call the North Carolina Autism Society (every state has one) for support and help in advocating for my daughter's Individualized Education Plan (IEP) in the school system. *Why do I need help?* I thought. *I can do that on my own. I am an educated person.* I soon learned that nothing could be further from the truth.

Connect Families with Support and Resources

In working with special-needs children and their families, one of the greatest things you can do is give special-needs families permission to seek support, then connect them with appropriate resources. Individual or family counseling alone will not be enough. Every state and community needs an organization like TEACCH. As a Christian counselor or caregiver, I encourage you to take time to get to know what is available in your area. If there aren't many resources, support groups, and educational classes for parents, consider partnering with other clinicians to make these available. Pray about how God would use you to raise awareness and provide support to families in your community with a special-needs child.

Reaching out for help is one of the best decisions I ever made. I realized quickly that the school system took advantage of my lack of knowledge of the laws concerning disabilities in school and simply wanted to label my daughter as a "conduct disordered" child and toss her in a BED/BEH (behavior focused classroom) room. I was in over my head. I called the NC Autism Society, became a member, and sought out help and support. I have no idea why I was embarrassed to admit I needed help with a disorder I knew nothing about, but I was.

An advocate came with me to a crucial IEP meeting, and as she spoke, quoted laws and mandates, and advocated for my child, I was so glad she was on my side! I was impressed. She fought to keep my child out of the secluded behavior-focused classroom and fought for us to get a shadow/aid for my daughter. Not only that, the advocate also did a demonstration in my daughter's class to help the students better understand my daughter's autism and her sensory needs. This normalized some things for her classmates and helped them understand what was going on when they saw her act out, throw a fit, or have a public meltdown.

The children who saw that demonstration never bullied my child again and seemed to give her grace when teachers and other adults could not. NC Autism Society helped me, supported me, and inspired me to advocate and speak up for other children. They helped empower me to do for others what they did for me.

As a counselor, I encourage you to tell your special needs' families to reach out, because getting adequate support is crucial to the health of the entire family. Visit Autism Speaks for a directory of available resources in your state.

Encourage Screening and Early Diagnosis

Many times, parents notice autistic-type behaviors but say, "We just don't want to label her," or, "We think he'll grow out of it," or, "We don't want her to feel different from the other kids." However, if a child is acting out at school or not excelling, the school system is already giving him a label of either "conduct issue" or "lazy."

Why not get the appropriate evaluation and get the *right* label? The child in question already knows she is different, so why not celebrate that difference and get the proper label so that the child can get the help they need at school, as well as other treatments and therapies? These may include occupational therapy, speech therapy, physical therapy, specialized diets, chelation, hippotherapy, vitamins and supplements, and more. I admit it can all be overwhelming, but early intervention and finding the right protocol for a child will be a worthwhile investment.

Unfortunately, the school system is not always a child's advocate, so parents must step up to the plate. Often, classes are overcrowded and teachers are overworked. However, there are programs in place to help special-needs children … but parents must take the initiative to seek them out. With the help of advocates and support, my husband and I fought for what our daughter needed. Today, she is very successful in a mainstream class gifted program at our local public school.

Life in the Trenches

From our own experience, as well as working with other families, I have three main pieces of advice:

- Encourage families to reach out for help, and connect them with appropriate resources and support groups in the local community.
- Encourage screening and early diagnosis whenever autism spectrum disorder is suspected, in order to gain access to needed treatments and therapy.
- Help parents advocate for their child in school and capitalize on their strengths, wherever they are on the spectrum.

The journey is not easy, by any means. That's why no family should do it alone. My daughter went from an autism-secluded classroom to a mainstream class with a shadow/aid, to a behavior-focused class, to home school, to a two-teacher team in mainstream, to a regular mainstream class.

There have been many struggles and trials along the way, but when I look at where she is now, I am eternally grateful for the people God placed in our life to educate us about autism, connect us with resources, and help us advocate for our daughter. Will you be that for someone else?

APPENDIX IV

Autism Awareness:
Should I Tell My Child She Is On the Spectrum?
Stephanie C. Holmes, M.A., BCCC
Certified Autism Specialist

One in fifty. That's the newly released estimate of school-aged children who are on the autism spectrum. One of the questions I'm most often asked is, "Should I tell my child that they are different from other children? Should I tell them about their diagnosis?" Many parents fear labeling their child and the stigma associated with diagnostic labels. Although I understand these fears, we live in a world of labels, and I explain to parents, "Your child is different and because of that people around him or her are going to label them. I would prefer they get the correct label."

What If My Child Is Labeled?
Often, children on the spectrum who are not diagnosed or not labeled will be victim to misinterpretations of their behaviors and mannerisms by the adults in charge. It is a fact of life that a child who has learning challenges or who is on the spectrum will not receive the help that can be provided through a 504 plan or Individualized Education Plan (IEP) without the proper diagnostic label.

One educational website shares: "Only certain classifications of disability are eligible for an IEP, and students who do not meet those classifications but still require some assistance to be able to participate fully in school would be candidates for a 504 plan." Disabilities or challenges that meet the requirements for service are specifically outlined. The school system is not required to give services based on a parent's hunch or because a child is failing school or has various behaviors of concern. In order for the school to put a plan in place, the label or diagnosis is required.

What If My Child Is Treated Differently?
Understandably, many parents share, "I don't want my child to feel that he or she is different. I don't want them to be treated differently." I can tell you that your child will eventually figure out

that they are different, that they are "differently abled." My concern is when a child on the spectrum is in a school setting and is not diagnosed, teachers form other labels like, "disruptive," "defiant," "lazy," "difficult," "selfish," "rude," or, "does not belong in this classroom."

That is why I say I prefer that children to get the proper label. Eventually, the child will figure out that they are different. I like to take a proactive approach with my children and let them know that they are different, and different does not mean bad or less than. Different can be good.

Our Family's Story

When I told my daughter she had Asperger's Syndrome, she was in the fourth grade. I wanted her to know that *autism* was only one label or word that describes her behavior. These are the labels I described to my daughter. I said, "Sydney, I want to explain to you why you have been having such a hard time at school and making friends, but before I do I want to tell you some very important things about yourself."

"First of all, you are a child of God. You are made in His image and here are some things the Bible says about that. It means you are:

- loved (John 3:16).
- chosen (I Thessalonians 1:4).
- a new creation (2 Corinthians 6:13).
- blessed (Galatians 3:9).
- victorious (Revelation 12:11).
- an heir in Christ (John 17:11).
- fearfully and Wonderfully Made (Psalm 139:14).
- forgiven (Ephesians 1:7)."

I took the time to read these verses to her and speak them over her. I further explained:

"You are not only a child of God, but you are my child and I love you unconditionally. There is nothing you can do that will make me not love you. I will defend you and protect you at school and anywhere because you are forever my child.

"You are gifted and talented in music and art. You have a loving heart for animals.

"You may not know how to tell people that you love them, but I know that in your heart, you love people and you try to help people in your way.

"You are a wonderful reader. You are gifted in math and science. You are so many wonderful things. These things are who you are.

"But you know how you have had struggles at school, how you keep getting in trouble, and you have trouble making friends? That is because you have something called *autism*. Autism makes it difficult for your brain to understand some things, and it is why you get frustrated sometimes and things bother you so easily. That is autism.

"I will never allow you to use autism as an excuse to fail. I will never allow you to use autism as an excuse for bad behavior. I will also remind you that you have Asperger's, but you get to decide if Asperger's has you. Asperger's is a condition you have.

"It does not have to define who you are, because you are so many other wonderful things. Asperger's causes some things to be hard, but it has some gifts, too, like your memory for details, your ability to solve math, and your wonderful vocabulary."

How Sydney Responded

"What did your daughter do about her diagnosis?" some people ask. "How did she take it?" These thoughts have been reinforced for the past five years. Let me share the essay Sydney just wrote for her ninth-grade composition. Her prompt was, "Write about a core belief that you hold dearly and be willing to share with the class." Below is that 500-word essay:

"People all over the world face challenges, struggles, and difficulties. The question is: Will they let that obstacle define them, or will they rise to overcome what was thought to be impossible? Many believe actions are set in stone, and it is not possible to overcome. There are few who do not. I believe that no matter who you are or what you have done, anyone can overcome an obstacle. No matter how hard, how difficult, or how impossible it seems, anyone can overcome an obstacle.

"There was this girl I used to know, who was very close to me. She had trouble in school, with friends, and nearly every aspect of her social life. This is because she has Asperger's Syndrome, also known as very high-functioning autism. When she was first diagnosed, the diagnosis was believed to be more prevalent in boys. Few teachers and few administrators knew how to help this girl succeed in school. The special education room was not a proper fit, but she found it difficult to be in the mainstream classroom. When she was confused or having an emotional meltdown, the teachers misinterpreted this behavior as disrespectful or disobedient behavior.

"In reality, she was communicating she needed help or further clarification of the instructions. Unfortunately, the girl was suspended for over fifty days of school and expelled from five schools by her third-grade year. Many people, including people her parents thought to be supportive family friends, gave up on her. They thought she would never overcome her problems or her struggles. They thought she was confined to a path [that] would lead to Juvenile Detention.

"This same girl who struggled so much in elementary school became an honor roll student throughout middle school. She is commonly referred to [now] as a 'goody two-shoes.'

"In case you have not put the pieces together, that girl was me. How is this possible? Well, I refused to allow others to define me by my behavior and my diagnosis. I was determined to prove to the teachers and the adults around me that their beliefs about me were wrong. I overcame my problems. My faith helped me overcome one struggle at a time. I decided that my diagnosis was not an excuse to fail. I will have to deal with more in my life than my fellow peers, but I refuse to let my problems limit who I can become.

"I hope that when my family has finalized adoption that I can help the children who come into our home to believe in themselves. Children in the foster care system have had many struggles and have had many people give up on them. I believe that my story can inspire them to believe that their past does not define who they can become. Nothing is impossible when you set your mind to achieve what you believe."

Do not be afraid of labels. Diagnostic labels can help you help your child get the services they need. Remind them of who they are, not what they have.

APPENDIX V

Adolescence

Adolescence is a challenging time whether or not you have a diagnosis of autism spectrum disorder/Asperger's. Spectrum teens certainly have a few more challenges to face during this already tumultuous stage of life than their non-spectrum counterparts. At the 2014 AACC National Conference in Branson, I taught a workshop on Autism Spectrum Disorder in Teens: Responding to Bullying, Depression, and Suicidal Ideation. During this time, my fifteen-year-old daughter, Sydney, helped me put together an interview to help show from an Aspie's perspective what life is like as a teenager.

A Research Update

Currently the rate of ASD diagnosis is ten to one, boys to girls. However, experts in the field including Dr. Tony Attwood, Dr. Temple Grandin, and Jennifer O-Toole believe this ratio is wrong. They believe the ratio is closer to four to one, boys to girls. Girls tend to be misdiagnosed or missed altogether because their brain wiring helps them at times to be less conspicuous.

In August 2013, research by the Autism Research Center at the University of Cambridge used MRIs to compare male and female ASD brains. Some notable results of the study include:

- As expected the tests found that the brain anatomies of females with autism were substantially different when compared to the brains of their male counterparts. In fact, a completely different set of regions were implicated in the male autism brain than in female autism brains.
- In terms of brain morphology, females with autism look more alike to typical developing males when compared to typical developing females.
- So, the brain changes in females with ASD are actually shifting toward typical developing males.

Recent research has also discovered differences in brain wiring of those who were formerly diagnosed with Asperger's Syndrome

179

when compared to autism.

One Teen's Perspective

It is easy to see how a female Aspie might have some additional challenges because her brain anatomy tends to develop more like a "neurotypical" male. This is very important to understand, and please note that this is not suggesting gender identity issues as far as sexuality. Often, though, secular therapists do try to convince female Aspies that they are transgender or lesbian simply because their thinking patterns and style of clothing may not be "female neurotypical," which can create confusion in the Aspie female.

I asked my daughter to share some challenges she has faced as a female on the Spectrum:

"Hi, my name is Sydney, and I am a fifteen-year-old girl in the tenth grade, and I have Asperger's Syndrome. My mom tells me they don't use that term any more, but I still prefer it. Where do I start? One of the common issues I am told is not "normal" for girls is that I could care less about my appearance. I *hate* fixing my hair and refuse to wear make-up. If I have to wear my hair in a ponytail, my scalp and hair hurt when I take it out of the ponytail. I hate having my hair curled and despise wearing any hair clips because they feel like they will fall out, and I don't like how they feel on my head. I sometimes will tolerate having my hair straightened, but I still hate feeling the heat so close to my face. I hate the way styling my hair feels.

"Another shocker is, even though I am a teenage girl, I *hate* shopping. Yes, I hate shopping for clothes and, apparently, this is something girls my age think is fun? Shopping has no point at all. I think it is ridiculous that a shirt or something will cost more just because it has a name brand on it; I mean you can get a similar shirt at Walmart for what—five dollars or eight dollars? Having said that, there is only really one type of clothes I wear. It is a name brand, ironically, but I do not like it because of the brand, I like it because the clothes are soft and more comfortable to wear. Some types of fabric are itchy or too thick or just don't feel right. Once I find a brand that feels good, I want to keep wearing that. Shopping and trying on clothes just for the sake of trying on clothes is a pointless ritual that girls my age do!

"My mom has explained that to be part of the group sometimes I have to go shopping, which is something I don't usually like. Sometimes, I go and I am like, 'Hey, while y'all try on clothes, I will hold your purses for you.' Then, I don't get stuck trying things on or having to comment on what they are trying on. Apparently, when a friend asks you, 'How do I look in this?' they are not usually asking for an honest answer. This also causes me stress, because I don't want to lie and tell them it looks nice when it doesn't, but apparently I am 'too honest.' I am also told I don't know when to stop explaining something.

"To be honest, I find it easier to hang out with the guys at my school. Guys are just simpler to hang out with. I may not always know what they are talking about, but they are less critical and don't talk about clothes, make-up, what actor married who, or teeny-bopper music. So, I guess it seems like I am not like other girls. This doesn't mean I don't want to have friends that are girls. I do. But it is hard to just hang out with girls because they want to talk about random, pointless things, and I am not usually interested in what they want to say.

"If I hang out with the guys, because they are less stressful, I may get accused of flirting or trying to talk to someone's boyfriend, and this is *not* the case. I feel like I am constantly in a catch-22 in most social situations at school. It's easier to hang out with friends one-on-one, or friends who know about my Asperger's who let me just be me."

That is just the tip of the iceberg, but as you are reading this and smiling and perhaps even laughing out loud at some of her thoughts, can you imagine how difficult is for her to relate to others her age? If you're interested in learning more about Aspie girls, I encourage you to check out a great article by advocate, author, and Aspie, Jennifer-O-Toole. At a conference presentation in 2013, Jennifer said that other concerns for Aspie girls include being at high-risk for anorexia, clinical depression, a victim of bullying, and commonly involved in a relationship where there is domestic violence.

There is growing literature about spectrum teens and spectrum girls, and it is my hope that there will be Christian counselors and coaches across the country who are equipped to offer excellent care and counsel in the midst of confusing messages the world so often gives to spectrum teens.

APPENDIX VI

Has Your ASD/SPD Client or Child Turned into the "Grinch"?

Stephanie C. Holmes, M.A., BCCC, Certified Autism Specialist

We have all heard the expression, "the sights and sounds of Christmas." When I think of the Christmas season, I think about love, laughter, hugs, family gatherings, buying gifts, decorating, food, Christmas lights, and all the sights and sounds and aromas of Christmas.

Don't get me wrong, of course, Christmas is about the birth of our Savior, and He is the "Reason for the season," but there are many components to the Christmas season that are very, very sensory-related. This can be problematic for your client or your child who is on the autism spectrum or has been diagnosed with sensory processing disorder (SPD).

Sensory Aversive or Sensory Seeking?

Sensory issues are complex, and this simple definition does not do the issue justice, but sensory stimuli enter through our five senses, and, for those who have sensory processing issues, their brains do not process the information the same way the neurotypical brain does. I call this the problem of "too." Sensory issues are real to ASD/SPD persons—they are not just making it up to be difficult.

As my daughter would commonly say, that is "too loud," or "too bright," or "too scratchy," or "too spicy," or "too" something. Sensory issues have two broad categories with many subcategories, but a person diagnosed with a sensory issue can be sensory aversive or sensory seeking. The aversive person is the person that will tend to use the word "too." That new sweater grandma gave me is "too itchy," or "too lacy," or "too red," or that new hair bow hurts my head, or that food is "too spicy."

As a parent, until I understood the complexities of sensory issues I thought, *Man she complains about everything! She has to be one of the most ungrateful children on the planet.* There is a sensory seeking side, as well. The sensory seeker loves to feel things, touch it all, see the bright lights and is enticed by sensory overload, but this overload then is followed by hyperactivity or a sensory crash. So, one child who is aversive may hate going to see the Christmas lights, talking to Santa, or being in a mall with throngs of people, while the sensory seeking child gets completely energized and hyperactive in the same situation.

It's All About the Brain

Two of the brain-based issues at work here are the corpus callosum and the amygdala. In the ASD brain, the amygdala is 15 to 20 percent larger than average. In simple terms, this part of the brain sizes up what is a threat and is involved in "fight or flight." Part of the issue with sensory integration is that the amygdala sizes up many sensory things as a threat, which causes the person to go into fight or flight. To the average onlooker, the person appears to be having a tantrum or at best is a "fussy child."

The corpus callosum is smaller in the ASD brain. A 2006 *TIME* magazine article reports, "The ASD corpus callosum works more like an improv jam session, instead of a beautiful orchestra." So sensations are not always accurately communicated across the brain hemispheres. One of best the ways to help ASD/SPD clients is by teaching them to regulate sensory issues. When a child with sensory issues is over-stimulated, there will be meltdowns, crankiness, irritability, anxiety, or ADHD-type behaviors. This time of year can really seem to turn your ASD/SPD client, or child, into the Grinch!

Easy Preventative Measures

I like to encourage people to be preventative and creative. First, assess what things tend to trigger the child. Work with the family to help them take some of the following actions. If the lights are too bright at the Christmas light show, the parents can let their child take some shades. If the sounds are an issue, parents can take some earmuffs and a device that plays music the child likes. Parents can talk to relatives ahead of time about gifts for the child to avoid embarrassing moments. Parents can explain the sensory issues and give some appropriate gift ideas. It also is important to practice with the child what is the appropriate thing to say or do if offered a food or gift they do not like.

If hugs are an issue and the parents know that Aunt Helen loves those hugs and kisses, talk with the child about what they might feel is an OK greeting—one hug, an air hug, a hand shake, etc. Encourage the parents to explain to the touchy-feely aunt that this is the way she can express a greeting and that squeezy hugs or a dozen kisses are going to cause an issue.

One of the best resources for an ASD/SPD child is a great occupational therapist (OT). OTs are experts in helping you assess the exact sensory issues and how to better regulate them. Sensory issues and how to manage them can be a huge key to the child's success.

If you are looking for further educational resources, take a look at the free video at aspergerexperts2.com, which was created by two young men with Asperger's. From their own experience, they explain the number one thing we can do to help those on the spectrum. Hint? Help them regulate those sensory issues! After Christmas, we head into New Year's parties and then Valentine's. There is always a sensory overload holiday right around every corner, but as a Christian counselor, you can make a difference.

Reprinted with permission from Autism/Asperger's Digest.

APPENDIX VII

Asperger's and Aggression

Stephanie C. Holmes, M.A., Certified Autism Specialist

Note: This blog was posted after the December 14, 2012, school shooting at Sandy Hook Elementary School in Newtown, Connecticut.

I want to begin this blog by firmly stating that Asperger's or any other neurological or mental disorder is not a plausible excuse for the senseless murders of the innocent children and adults in Newtown, Connecticut. As a mother, therapist, minister, and American citizen, my heart aches for the tragic loss of lives at Sandy Hook Elementary School. However, as a mother of a teen with Asperger's, my heart also aches for Nancy Lanza, a victim and the mother of the shooter.

As I read stories about Nancy, she is said to have been kind, compassionate, and very involved in the lives of her children. MSN.com reported, "Friends had met Lanza's younger son, who stared down at the floor and didn't speak when she brought him in. They knew he'd switched schools more than once and that she'd tried homeschooling him. But while she occasionally expressed concern about his future during evenings at the bar, she never complained about anything at all."

As the story of this massacre in Newtown unfolds, the fact that Adam Lanza, the shooter, had been diagnosed with Asperger's keeps making the news. Some reporters are careful to say that most people with Asperger's are not prone to such violent acts, but other stories draw comparison to the Colorado movie theatre shooter James Holmes, who is also thought to have Asperger's. This raises an important question: Are individuals with Asperger's prone to violent acts and murder? What is the relationship between Asperger's and aggression/violence?

Understanding Autistic Aggression

An assistant professor of pediatrics and psychology at Ohio University, Eric Butter shares, "Aggression that we see in autism can best be described as disruptive and irritable behavior and is often consistent with the communication and social difficulties that are the hallmarks of autism spectrum disorders. It is a very human experience that when you cannot explain how you are feeling, that you will then act out in frustration, anger, and aggression. But it is not consistent with the diagnosis that you would plan and execute a crime like we saw here."

Aggression that leads to this kind of planned, violent, criminal act is not mentioned as a symptom in the current DSM-IV-TR or the new DSM-V. Eric Butter points out that, while between 20 and 30 percent of persons with autism act out aggressively, the aggression is usually a reaction or impulsive outburst. The autistic individual may be quick to shout in anger, push, shove, or throw something, but methodical planning of murderous acts is not related to the spectrum.

As the mother of a child with Asperger's, I am beginning to be concerned about prejudice toward persons with ASD because of the two massacres that occurred in 2012, within a six-month period, wherein the shooter was believed to be on the autism spectrum. It is important to remember that having one disease or disorder does not preclude an individual from having other disorders that could significantly affect functioning. For example, a person with cancer could also have another medical issue, such as diabetes or heart disease. The same is important to remember with a person on the autism spectrum.

Distinguishing Between Autism and Mental Illness

Autism spectrum disorder is not a mental illness. This point cannot be made strongly enough. It is currently under the heading "pervasive development disorders," described as a neurological glitch in the brain. A person on the spectrum usually has another diagnosis co-morbid with ADHD, such as OCD or ODD. Some individuals even have co-morbid bipolar disorder or anti-social personality disorder.

Adam Lanza was described by former classmates as "painfully shy, socially awkward, and a little off." These characteristics describe the Asperger's individual. Yet, no one who knew him thought him to be capable of such a heinous crime. Whatever happened in Adam Lanza's mind that horrible day was not a result simply of his Asperger's.

We must be careful to protect those with ASD against prejudice that would suggest their ASD diagnosis predisposes them to violent crimes. According to Dr. Tony Attwood at an Asperger's conference recently held in Atlanta, the ASD individual is actually more prone to a depression attack that could result in suicide than in homicidal violence. Attwood said that these individuals can have a sudden "depression attack" that comes on quickly and strongly, as with a person who experiences a panic disorder. The depression attack can come with few warning signs; thus, cognitive therapy for Aspie teens is a proactive tool to combat such depression.

Another point Dr. Attwood made was that there is cause for concern when an individual with Asperger's develops a special interest in something like drugs, porn, or weapons. These are not common "special interests" among Aspie teens, but on rare occasions the Aspie can end up in trouble with the law when his or her special interest is something that is illegal. He spoke of his own son's interest in drugs, which eventually led him to serve jail time. It happens, but this is not the norm.

Treatment Options for ASD

As I read more about Nancy Lanza, I can't help but recognize a question that needs to be addressed more than gun control laws and the role of violent computer games: What is a parent to do when a teen or grown child with Asperger's or mental illness acts out and has an aggressive meltdown? Nancy Lanza's friends said she recently remarked she was afraid as Adam was getting older, she was "losing control of him."

What options are out there to help a parent when a child is acting out? I remember when my own child was in elementary school and was prone to aggressive meltdowns that resulted in her being put in holds, time-out closets, or held down by two or more adults. There was a time from first through third grade when we were concerned for the safety of classmates if my daughter had a meltdown and threw her pencil or scissors out of frustration. There was a time when we were concerned about leaving my daughter and her younger sister unattended for fear that she might do something to harm her sister unintentionally in a moment of rage.

As a mother, I wrestled with thoughts like, *Can I rear this child on my own? Does she need a specialized institution/program?* I can feel Nancy's pain as she must have faced similar concerns. It is being hypothesized that she was in the process of trying to get Adam committed, which could possibly have been a motive in the shooting. There were not, and still are not, many good options for those who are not wealthy enough to afford private or in-home care. In the education system, parents are given the choice of a specialized classroom for the severely autistic/mentally challenged or a specialized classroom that focuses on severe behaviors.

Neither of these are good options for the high-functioning ASD individual. These children usually have high intelligence and can learn. The challenge is finding the right environment to help them learn while protecting the safety of others. Our family's local school system actually recommended that I put my daughter in an institutionalized setting and give up parental rights until she was "under control." We did not have the funds for an in-home care specialist or a private facility. For us, like Nancy Lanza, one option was to homeschool and educate ourselves on all the available options and treatments.

What about when a behavior gets scary and out of control? Where do you turn? To have someone committed in a state institution, you have to prove that the person is homicidal or suicidal. Often with an individual on the spectrum, you do not get the suicidal clues that are a little more obvious with a neurotypical teen. Besides, a state mental facility is not necessarily the best placement for ASD children.

Parents and counselors must consider if an institutionalized environment may model more severe behaviors that the child does not yet possess. Aspies are great imitators. Juvenile detention and mental hospitals can sometimes exacerbate the problem by introducing more severe behaviors than the original meltdowns.

Helping Families with an ASD Child

Did you know that because Asperger's/ASD is not considered a medical disease or mental illness most insurance companies do not cover the various treatment options? Placement in private care or the hiring of an in-home specialist is usually not covered, either. What is a parent to do when he or she feels a symptom or behavior is becoming more than they can deal with?

With ASD growing to one out of eighty-eight children, and one out of fifty-four boys, what can be done to help families act preventively? There is a need for reform in mental health to equip families to help their teen or young adult who needs additional care and intervention.

As we process this tragedy, we must avoid making assumptions about persons with neurological issues or mental illness. We must also remember that there are many incidents of heinous acts committed by persons without Asperger's and that Adam Lanza had more severe issues to contend with than simply ASD. As our nation mourns the loss of these innocent lives, we must avoid developing prejudice against children and adolescents with Asperger's/ASD. Instead, I challenge you to consider how you can support and help these individuals and their families.

APPENDIX VIII

Asperger's and Spirituality
Stephanie C. Holmes

As I recall a time in my daughter's life when she was not drawn toward the church or Christians, I wonder how others with Asperger's Syndrome feel about the church, religion, and spirituality. So, I Googled Asperger's and religion to research Aspies' thoughts about this matter. (Individuals with Asperger's often refer to themselves as Aspies). To my surprise, there are hundreds of articles written about Aspies and religion. *Psychology Today* recently featured two articles on this very topic: "Bullying, Hypocrisy, and Church: An Asperger Perspective on Religion," and "The Pain of Isolation: Asperger's and Suicide."

The reality of many Aspies' experience with religious hypocrisy grieves me. Aspies are known to be literal, black and white thinkers who want or need evidence or proof. Spiritual faith does not require proof. Many are known for great intelligence, and Aspies tend to value knowledge and perfection. Aspies are also known to have narrow interests and can obsess about topics of interest to them. How would these tendencies relate to an interest in spirituality? I found articles by Aspies who not only report a deep connection to Christianity, but to many other religions, as well. However, many report rejecting faith, too.

Aspies have the ability to grasp spiritual concepts and to develop a personal relationship with God, but relationships can be a challenge, if not an enigma, in the Aspie mind. Aspies are not known for their social skills, relationship building, or affect recognition, but I can tell you they are usually quite adept at detecting incongruences between one's stated beliefs and one's actual behavior.

As I read articles by Christian Aspies, I find that many have black and white beliefs about God, the Bible, and what behaviors are acceptable and which are not. Some confess to being overly perfectionistic or legalistic in their faith, but their understanding of God and His Word is real. I can see this in my own daughter's understanding of these matters. She, too, can be quite legalistic in her faith and get caught up in what Robert McGee's *Search for Significance* calls, "the performance trap."

For example, she can become easily stressed if she receives money and forgets to tithe on it the very first Sunday she has the opportunity. She can raise money for missions and have a thought that she wished she had raised the money for herself and feel overly guilty for having a natural human thought. This is a wonderful teaching moment as I try to guide my daughter through her now teenage faith.

In her childhood, she experienced some things that made her feel disconnected from church. When she was mistakenly expelled from the Christian school associated with our home church after being promised, "We are your church. We love you. We will never expel you," she called the headmaster and staff pastor a liar.

She screamed, "The church lies. He did not love me for who I was." She carried bitterness and hurt from that experience for nearly four years. Thankfully, she remained tender toward God, but she had a negative feeling about "the church" as an institution. This is just one example of literal, black and white thinking.

I wish my daughter's experience was an isolated incident. But, as I read articles about children and adult Aspies, many are quick to point out the hypocrisy in the church. It seems these individuals have paid attention to the sermons about how Christians are called to live and what the Bible calls sin. To individuals with Asperger's, the biggest proof for the nonexistence of God is when they see people in the pew living double lives. For a black and white, literal, visual proof thinker, one negative interaction with a "Christian" can cause them to write off spirituality all together.

In my review of what Aspies have written about spirituality and religion, it seems the most common stumbling block is a negative experience with Christians. Aspies usually want to have contact and relationships with others. However, they lack many of the social skills required to keep such a relationship. Many individuals with Asperger's believe that, since their schools, jobs, or peers have rejected them or made fun of them, surely the church will be a place to find solace and understanding. After all, the Bible commands us to love God, to love people and to follow the golden rule. This sounds like a welcome refuge to individuals who are often socially rejected, misunderstood and ostracized. But too many times, Aspies experience the same rejection in the church.

This reported rejection by their peers and "places of refuge" could explain the research that reports that, by the age of thirteen, nearly 50 to 60 percent of Aspies have contemplated suicide. This is double the national norm of non-Asperger teens. Research shows that the rate of suicides among Aspies is on the rise. When Aspies are asked why they contemplate suicide, the most common response is the pain of isolation and rejection.

Jesus said in John 13:35, "Your love for another will prove you are My disciples." For an Aspie, this could quite literally mean a meaningful relationship with God and other believers, or rejection of God and disconnection with His people. Sadly, it could be a life and death decision. The stakes are high.

Will we be the Church? Will we reach out to individuals with Asperger's and seek to understand them? Or will we reject them because of their odd behaviors and our own discomfort interacting with them? As counselors and ministers, we must take the lead in living out the Gospel in such a way that we offer hope, acceptance, and safe relationships to those who are different from us, including those with Asperger's.

APPENDIX IX

The Growing Concern of Suicide and High-Functioning Autism

Stephanie C. Holmes, MA, BCCC, Certified Autism Specialist

How many suicides are enough to warrant concern that there is a problem in this country with our suicide rate?

Just one. One should be enough to make us pause and wonder why someone would feel that suicide was the best solution to his or her situation. There are 30,000 deaths every year in this country due to suicide.

Every seventeen minutes a suicide is completed and every forty-two seconds someone is attempting suicide. Studies show 80 to 90 percent of those who commit suicide had a mental health issue. The rates of suicide are rising among teens with high functioning autism (formerly called Asperger's/Aspies). There is not a study to provide empirical numbers, but those working with Aspie teens are suggesting that 50 percent of Aspie teens have contemplated or attempted suicide and Aspie teens are at a 40 to 50 percent higher risk of completing suicide than their neurotypical (NT) counterparts.

Consider these two scenarios:

Zach (not his real name), age eighteen, is an honor student about to be inducted into a national honor society. Lately, his family feels he has been turning some poor choices around and for once he is really talking about college and pursuing a choice career. There have been no changes in his friend circles, no talk of depression in the past three to four months. Things seem to be looking up! The future is bright. The family couldn't be prouder of his high school and fencing achievements.

Susie (not her real name) is a thirteen-year-old eighth grader. She makes all As, and everyone around her tells her of her beauty and intelligence. She has a few good friends and is one of the teacher's favorites. There has been some middle school girl drama and some ups and downs in friendships. Recently, a mean girl targeted her to exclude her from a group going on a school trip that she had highly anticipated since sixth grade. Her family is concerned about the exclusion/bullying and asked her how she was doing processing all of this. She gave all the right answers, her grades never dropped, and her routine did not change.

Which student would you be more concerned about contemplating or completing suicide? We are taught that the common markers are the onset of depression, talking about death or wishing they had never been born, giving away treasured items, talk of actual plans, acute anxiety, or changes in friends or routines. What if the parent of each were concerned and went to mental health providers but were turned away? What if these students came to you as a counselor or minister? Do they present as suicide risk?

The answer to the question as to which one was at higher risk is—both! Both students were diagnosed with Asperger's. "Susie" attempted and daydreamed about suicide but did not complete the action. Zach, unfortunately, successfully took his life this year.

What makes an Aspie teen at higher risk? The number one reason is social isolation and/or rejection, which lowers an already low self-esteem. What adds to this feeling of rejection is that many times Aspies do have decent friendships and get invited to parties in elementary school, then there is sudden shift in middle school.

Middle school is the time the teen notices he or she is "different." Other students seem to notice it too. Those who had been friends in elementary school suddenly distance themselves. This is confusing for the Aspie. "Why were we friends in fifth grade but not sixth grade? What did I do? How can I make them like me again?"

A blog called "Your Little Professor" said:

"In the teenage world where everyone feels insecure, teens that appear different are voted off the island. Aspies often have odd mannerisms. One teen talks in a loud unmodulated voice, avoids eye contact, interrupts others, violates the physical space of others, and constantly steers the topic of conversation to his or her favorite odd topic."

Sometimes these teens appear aloof, cold, and selfish or like they "want to be loners." Adolescence is a time students are seeking identity and peer approval. What is one to do when all attempts to make friends result in being shunned or bullied?

What else in changing in middle school? Schoolwork is getting harder. The "hand holding" and encouragement many received in elementary school is no longer the case in middle school. School expectations are different. Students are expected to do public presentations and, worse for Aspies, group projects. When teachers allow the students to pick their own groups, guess who is often left out and then has to reluctantly form what gets referred to as the "loser group" with the others that were also not included.

We have all heard of "anxiety attacks" but Dr. Tony Attwood said Aspie teens are prone to "depression attacks." An Aspie teen can wake up fine in the morning exhibiting no signs of anxiety or depression and have a trigger at school, such as being bullied, getting a low grade on an assignment, getting a feeling that a teacher does not like them, breaking up with a friend, and suddenly be under what he calls a "depression attack."

The depression comes on intensely and, paired with a pre-frontal cortex that does not always see permanent consequences of actions, is not getting a "do not do it" message from the executive part of their brain. They see the suicide as an immediate response to end sudden, intense pain, and thoughts of it being something that cannot be undone is not usually part of their pre-frontal cortex thinking process.

Attwood adds that inherent to the condition is the tendency to catastrophize. Because of this tendency, there are challenges to regulate their emotions. Add to that the fact that the amygdala of an Aspie tends to be 10 to 15 percent larger than in neurotypicals, which can inflate the "danger alerts" in the fight/flight/freeze system. What would have been a one on the scale for an NT individual could easily have registered as a 10 to the Aspie.

The overactive amygdala sends signals that start the heart racing, adrenaline production, stomach churning, and as Attwood said, "It is like the Aspie is the last to know about his or her heightened emotions. He appears to be just as surprised as the observer when emotions have escalated." He added that in addition to an enlarged amygdala there is less white fiber between amygdala and frontal lobe. The frontal lobes are not getting the signals that the system is under duress and there is little interaction from the executive function, which in NTs would be saying, "Calm down, hitting them will get you in trouble. Breaking that is not a good idea."

Aspies have made an art form of "making a mountain out of a molehill" to many people, but what we need to understand is that what may be a molehill to one *is* a mountain to the Aspie. I agree with Dr. Attwood that cognitive-behavioral therapy is crucial for Aspie teens to get often. We should not wait until we think the teen has exhibited something to "need" therapy.

A good therapist who understands Asperger's and issues of adolescence can help the teen explore various issues before it is a major problem. Attwood said that Aspie teens should be getting regular "mental health checkups" to help navigate the tumultuous times of adolescence as preventive measures to help with "depression attacks" and learn positive self-talk and recognize catastrophizing before they take a permanent action for a temporary problem.

I urge therapists and ministers to take time to understand high functioning autism (Asperger's). It appears to be becoming a matter of life and death in this population of teens.

APPENDIX X

Asperger's and Marriage: Therapy that Works
Stephanie C. Holmes

One area of Asperger's (soon to be included in autism spectrum disorder) that is woefully behind in research and resources is the subject of Aspie marriages. Asperger's and marriage? Wait a minute. Perhaps you've been taught that Aspies prefer solitude and do not usually seek out lifelong relationships. Maybe you have heard the myth that Aspies are somehow doomed to lives of "less than" when it comes to friendships or marital relationships.

Since Asperger's was first acknowledged in the Diagnostic and Statistical Manual-IV in 1994, there has been an explosion of research and articles about raising someone on the spectrum, Aspies and school issues, and everything you need to know about social skills with Aspie kids. Guess what? Those early Aspies diagnosed in the 1990s are not children anymore. Many people with Asperger's Syndrome did (and do) marry. What about people who had Aspie qualities before the 1990s, before the term Asperger's came on the therapy scene?

What are some blind spots of persons with Asperger's that might challenge the marriage relationship?

Emotional intimacy. Social skills. Empathy skills. Mind blindness. Finances. Money spent on special interests. You may think of these as normal marriage challenges; however, these areas tend to be exacerbated when a person is on the spectrum. Verbal or physical aggression can occur if a daily routine is blocked or something does not go as planned.

Many people report coming away from their first encounter with an adult Aspie with one of many commonly held misperceptions—they are selfish, cold, rude, stubborn, egotistical, uncaring, callous, or unsocial. The frustrating thing for those of us who love someone on the spectrum is that we know these attributes are not true. Many times the Aspie is not even aware they are coming across to others that way. But, if a spouse interprets a behavior with one of these notions, a marriage relationship could be greatly challenged.

How often do therapists misunderstand or misdiagnose Asperger's in adults?

As I reflect on recent contact from those who have had adult children and/or spouses with Asperger's Syndrome, I am sad to report many individuals were frustrated and hurt by therapists, simply because the therapist did not fully understand how Asperger's impacts relationships. Many of the normal techniques and theories applied to marriage and family counseling are not as effective when applied to persons on the spectrum and often leave the clients confused and hurt.

Because of a late diagnosis in life and trying to understand more about who they are, more and more adults with Asperger's are seeking counseling. Usually, the impetus for that search is related to marital or vocational stress as a result of some of the Aspie's blind spots. Persons married to an Aspie are seeking help to better understand their Aspie spouse and strategies to live in peace while still having their own emotional needs met. This can be a tall order when the spouse is neurologically challenged in the areas of empathy and intimacy. To further complicate the matter, it is not uncommon for the Aspie spouse to get the diagnosis later in life because of a child in the diagnosis process of autism spectrum disorder. Sadly, divorce is becoming commonplace in Aspie marriages because many couples don't know how to cope.

What approach tends to be the most successful for Aspie marriage counseling?

Individuals with Asperger's tend to stay cognitive. Issues of emotions concerning how others feel and interpreting events are major issues for them because of mind blindness. (Mind blindness is sometimes called the opposite of empathy. It is the inability to understand how another may be feeling or processing emotions.) Aspies tend to be straightforward people, and they will not stay in therapy if they do not see how they will achieve results.

Cognitive-Behavioral Therapy (CBT) with a little dose of explanation of Family Systems seems to be the most effective approach. Dr. Tony Attwood explained recently at a conference held in Atlanta, "These individuals rarely know how they feel most of the time, much less how others feel. They also tend to think others think like them. Asking them a question about how someone else might feel about that is a completely foreign concept to them."

Approaches that are emotionally based are frustrating and painful for Aspies; however, good, solid logic and explanation of consequences of various behaviors—and how those behaviors affect the spouse and the family—can connect with their 1+1=2 mentality.

Sharing stories or actual events are also usually effective. Remember, in children's therapies, social stories are often used to teach children and adolescents new social skills. Sharing stories of marital success and failures, with practical guidelines on how to achieve success and avoid failure, provides a road map for Aspies to learn new strategies. Most Aspies are loyal and do seek to please the one they love. However, many times they are stuck on how to demonstrate their love or how their actions or words affect the other person.

What will help us conceptualize marriage challenges for Aspies?

Some resources for Aspie marriages advise that you look at the Aspie and neurotypical (NT) partners as being from two different cultures. Each partner needs to better understand the other's "culture" and ways of communication. After a better understanding of how each person processes and responds, the couple can be guided into techniques and tools that will aid them in better communication patterns. Hence, this is why CBT and Family Systems work tends to be the best strategy for couples. The Aspie wants to please their spouse, and if you are able to logically connect with the Aspie client and help them navigate the NT world, they are usually responsive. These skills will not come naturally, but Aspies can be taught various social cues and interpersonal skills.

There is so much more to cover about how Aspies "do marriage," but I want to emphasize that Aspies can have lasting, fulfilling marriages, and although some marital strategies may be different than the norm, part of helping the Aspie marriage is understanding how Asperger's impacts the marriage and which strategies can bring help to the marriage.

APPENDIX XI

Asperger's and Emotions:
Effective Interventions for Counselors
Stephanie C. Holmes, M.A., Certified Autism Specialist

Understanding an Aspie's Emotions

Role reversal strategies and re-enacting various scenes at home are not effective with Aspies. Do not tell them to "think like their spouse." Do not ask them, "What would your spouse feel or think if you did that?" or "How would you feel if that were said to you?" These questions make no sense to them. A good rule of thumb when working with emotions is to encourage Aspie spouses to try to "think outside of themselves."

An adult client I recently worked with explained it like this:

> "You know those cones of water that dump out at water parks? The cone is upside down and eventually is filled with water. One last drop enters the cone, and the cone suddenly spills over and dumps the water on the head of the one underneath and then flips immediately back over to begin being filled again. That is how my emotions work. I am completely unaware that the emotion is filling up on the inside. I am unaware when I am at a flipping over level. My spouse thinks that the last little thing was the trigger to the emotional meltdown, but the truth is I had no idea I was so stressed or upset until the last 'drop' happened and it caused me to spill all the emotion out on her."

Work or other stressors could have been building for a month, and one little thing said by a spouse triggered the verbal meltdown. The Aspie is then confused on how big the emotions seem to get so quickly and unaware that his reaction was hurtful to the spouse. He might respond something like this, "She should have known that was not directed at her. She shouldn't get her feelings hurt so easily." This is not typically the response an offended spouse wants to hear.

Monitoring Body and Emotional States

Helping an adult with Asperger's learn how to monitor their body and emotional states is a huge skill that will help relieve this stress in their marriage. Helping them understand how their body tends to over-react to the fight, flight, and freeze responses is a useful tool to the Aspie. These individuals are not usually aware of signals their body is giving them to indicate that they are experiencing a heightened emotion. Use of facial emotions and having the spouse show the Aspie individual what their face looks like at various times will help them understand what the spouse is experiencing.

Aspies do not tend to see the signs of anxiety such as racing heart, or sweaty palms, or being easily agitated as their autonomic nervous system is being aroused. It is a good idea to educate them about anxiety and teach techniques that can reduce anxiety. The spouse of the Aspie also needs to learn the body language of when "the cone is filling up," so they know how to navigate some of their timing and responses. It becomes important to recognize facial and body cues that suggest the Aspie spouse is close to emotional meltdown. In therapy, the spouse can come to understand and begin to put into words what they are experiencing.

Star Trek and Aspie Relationships

With no disrespect intended to Aspies, the way I explain some relational issues of Aspies to the non-Aspie or neurotypical (NT) spouse involves using two *Star Trek* characters. The first is Spock from the original *Star Trek* series. Spock was half-Vulcan and half-human. Spock's character was half of each race, but he was never really accepted or understood by either. The Vulcan race sought to live a life of reason and logic without interference of emotion because emotions are not logical or rational.

This is how the Aspie tends to process life. They are constantly trying to make sense out of life, processing what they are experiencing through their five senses, without much thought to emotion—theirs or others. This is not because they do not have emotion, but they are simply not aware it is there until it is too late, as in the "filled cone" analogy.

Aspies pride themselves on logic, rationality, and doing things efficiently. When this is challenged or if they feel they are being accused, they may be verbally curt or short with someone. If a spouse tries to use tears or strong emotion to sway their Aspie mate, this can be taken offensively or evoke confusing emotion in the Aspie, which may then be "spilled out" unexpectedly.

But Spock is only half of the picture.

Another character who can add to the analogy is Lieutenant Commander Data from *Star Trek: The Next Generation.* Data was an android who for many years did not contain an "emotion chip," and he was curious to know all he could about human emotion. His naiveté often got him in trouble in his interactions, especially with female characters. For example, if a female were to ask Data how she looked or his thoughts about her appearance, he might cock his head to the side, give a glance, then commence to explain what he saw in a straightforward way.

As the viewer, you would recognize the female's face was registering anger or embarrassment or frustration, yet these were not registering to Data as he would continue his analysis. If the female slapped him or cried or stormed off, he was left standing there dazed and then asked another character, "Why did she behave that way? I simply gave her the data she requested as to her appearance, and her response seems to be unwarranted by my honest response."

If you watched *Star Trek*, you knew Data's character was not malicious, cruel, or mean-spirited. He simply could not process what the other person wanted, and he did not have the communication skills of how to "bless someone's heart" as we say in the South, or gloss over the 100 percent honest answer and say something to make the other person feel better. He gave the answer to the question he was asked. This analogy usually helps the NT spouse understand.

Learning to Communicate in New Ways

If you are expecting platitudes or your Aspie spouse to somehow "know" you are seeking a compliment, it won't happen without cues. Aspies are not cruel or unkind with their words on purpose. They are sometimes like Commander Data, clueless as to what the response should be. So, I like to say, combine the logical processing of Spock and the sometimes clueless social skills of Data, and you can better understand why Aspies respond the way they do. Aspies fear saying or doing the wrong thing in social context, especially to the people they care about.

If the neurotypical spouse is upset and seeking comfort, asking a question to seek a compliment, or crying because something has upset them, the Aspie registers that their spouse is hurting, but does not always know how to respond. In Spock's way of not wanting to respond wrongly, they may choose not to respond at all, which appears cold and uncaring, but is merely self-protection on their part to avoid doing or saying the wrong thing. They may remain silent or offer logical, calculated advice. The response may be a social faux pas just as Data gave, but they will give the literal response in a genuine effort to help or answer. Often, however, they get a response they do not understand. As you can see, this is frustrating for both spouses.

Dr. Tony Attwood explains it this way to his male Aspie adults:

"Emotionally, you are like a cactus. You do not require a lot of watering by emotion and platitude. A drop of emotion or compliment goes a long way with you, just like water to a cactus. However, your NT partner is a delicate rose. She needs more water; that is, more attention and compliments than you do. Sometimes, you get confused; because you are a cactus you think others are designed that way, too. But NT's are more emotionally fragile and need some emotional 'watering,' even if you think it is unnecessary or excessive; different plants like roses need different types of care. If you were a gardener, you would learn what plant needs what to survive. If you want your spouse to bloom, she will need more from you in this area, even though it does not make logical sense to you."

APPENDIX XII

Did the DSM-5 Get It Right About Autism Spectrum Disorder?
Stephanie C. Holmes

There are two major things that have upset clinicians and educators who work with persons on the spectrum:

1. The removal of both PDDNOS and Asperger's Syndrome. Scientific studies reviewing and researching the new diagnostic terms show that it is these two groups of individuals that seem to be excluded from the new criteria. This is primarily problematic in services to be received in the school setting. For those previously diagnosed with PDDNOS or Asperger's who were receiving services, most are being "grandfathered in" to the ASD diagnosis and are still receiving services. The issue becomes the thousands who could have received services but now may be excluded with the new diagnostic criteria.

2. The change from three major criteria in DSM-IV-TR to two criteria in the DSM-5. In the previous manual, there were three criteria in which to judge if a person showed autistic characteristics: social skills, communication, and repetitive or restricted behaviors. In the new manual, there are now only two, as social skills and communication have been combined into one criteria. That may seem subtle, but that is a big change. Also, in the DSM-5 there is a stricter criteria for what meets the standard of a repetitive or restrictive behavior. This is also problematic because how one demonstrates their restrictive behavior may be dependent on their temperament, home environment, access to therapies, or current support in managing those behaviors.

The new manual did include a new diagnosis called social (pragmatic) communication disorder. It is thought many who previously qualified as Asperger's Syndrome or maybe even PDDNOS might better fit in this diagnosis. Here is how the manual explains it for us:

"Individuals with autism spectrum disorder may only display the restricted/repetitive patterns of behavior, interests, and activities during the early developmental period, so a comprehensive history should be obtained. Current absence of symptoms would not preclude a diagnosis of autism spectrum disorder, if the restricted interests and repetitive behaviors were present in the past. A diagnosis of social (pragmatic) communication disorder should be considered only if the developmental history fails to reveal any evidence of restricted/repetitive patterns of behaviors, interests, or activities."

So, the main difference is any developmental history of repetitive or restrictive behaviors. This can be problematic in getting the developmental history of a teenager or adult because often, higher-functioning individuals may have learned to manage the behaviors or develop more "socially acceptable" ones like Bible study, or rigid beliefs about morality, or cooking, or music composition. Not every restrictive interest is "autism stereotypical," as in interest in small parts, vehicles, rocks, or ceiling fans. Oftentimes, parents new to the process are not really sure what falls under that category because all kids as toddlers have some phase they are in—cars, Thomas the Tank Engine, Elmo, fairies, etc.

Caregivers may not always know when the pattern has crossed over into restrictive or repetitive. Some parents, when I interact with their child and they tell me their child cannot be autistic because they do not have any of those "behaviors," react when I point out behaviors I observe. The parents often respond that the behavior is just "quirky" or "a phase every child has."

So the criteria language and what that manifests can be troublesome if the clinician does not have a trained eye on the whole spectrum of autism. If they stick to literal terms as to what may be repetitive and restrictive, since parents are giving the history, those behaviors may be missed in the assessment.

Social communication and social skills are the same thing, right? According to the DSM-5, yes, but according to those who work with these individuals, there are nuances in one's ability to communicate and one's ability to know the right thing to do or say in the appropriate social situations. Oftentimes, those who were previously called Asperger's tend to be able to hold wonderful conversations (if the discussion is about their special interests) and thus appear completely neurotypical, but they may not know how to interact with a group of people at the church banquet or work Christmas party.

Around the world, the term *Asperger's* is still being used and scientific studies abound that indicate it should still be part of the spectrum as a distinctive sub-type. A study in the BMC Medicine journal, which compared EEGs of neurotypical and Asperger Syndrome children, found that "all the children with autism—including those with Asperger's—showed weaker connections in language associated regions of the brain's left hemisphere. However, the researchers found distinctively strong activity in other areas of the brain among those diagnosed with Asperger's Syndrome." The study showed these distinctively strong areas were not present in the normally developing child's brain.

As a clinician and a mother working in this field, I stay attentive to the research being done in other parts of the world concerning ASD/Asperger's Syndrome. When I speak, although it is now "clinically incorrect" in the United States, in my opinion it is more accurate to still use the distinction of Asperger's Syndrome. Organizations such as Emory Autism Center, Marcus Autism Center, and TEACCH still use the term, as well.

This article was certainly not meant to answer this heated debate, but to encourage clinicians to look beyond the language of the DSM-5 as you seek to provide excellent care to your clients and their families. I hope I have challenged us all to look for truth wherever it may be found, rather than limiting ourselves to one manual.

Endnotes:
Attwood, Tony (2012). Atlanta Autism Conference.

APPENDIX XIII

Complex Cases: Aspie-NT Marriage
Cassandra Phenomenon Ongoing
Traumatic Relationship Syndrome
Rev. Stephanie C. Holmes, MA, BCCC
Certified Autism Specialist

As my work with Aspie-NT couples has expanded now across the U.S. and other countries as a consultant, coach, or counselor, it is becoming clear to me that the Aspie-NT couple phenomenon is growing in numbers, and there is not significant growth in understanding and working with couples with this unique dynamic among secular or Christian counselors. I receive emails or Skype contacts, usually from a wife (in most cases who is the "neurotypical"/NT) who is desperate for help because a child is diagnosed or suspected of Autism Spectrum Disorder (ASD/Asperger's/High Functioning Autism) and perhaps, just perhaps, her husband is, as well. Current CDC statistics report in 2015 the rate of ASD is one out of sixty-eight children. As children are being diagnosed, it is becoming a common issue that a parent (usually, but not always, the father) becomes suspected of being on the spectrum as well. As some spouses say it, "I think my husband may have a touch of this," or, "I am not sure if he has all the traits but the diagnoses explains ... ." Usually, my first email contact from the spouse includes the question, "Is this narcissism or Asperger's/ASD?" (This question is addressed in a previous AACC blog "NPD or ASD?"). Since the term *Asperger's Syndrome* did not come upon the scene until 1994, does that mean it did not exist before 1994? Certainly not. So, what about persons who met the criteria well before 1994? Those individuals would be adults presently, often married and may already have children.

As I was perusing sites about Aspie-NT marriage, what is becoming clear and unsettling to me is an "US vs. THEM" mentality (NT vs. ASD). Blogs or sites that lean more heavily toward Aspie support can be quite harsh or terse about blaming the NTs as the results of all the issues that perplex or confuse or traumatize the

213

Aspie person comes to light. Sites that lean more heavily toward support of the NT can be quite vicious, cruel, and demeaning, or paint a picture of hopelessness for any kind of marital satisfaction with someone with ASD, or an Aspie. Let me be crystal clear that neither side is creating an accurate picture. I also want to address this "US vs. THEM" in a two-part series. This one will focus on the NT spouse, and the next will focus on Aspie/ASD issues in marriage as to give equal time to issues creating challenges and sometimes psychological trauma (for one or both spouses) in this complex marriage situation.

For those who are reading my work for the first time, please know I am not just a counselor/therapist who works with persons on the spectrum, I am the mother of someone on the spectrum, and I desire to write from both perspectives, as I am NT but deeply love and advocate for my own Aspie/ASD child.

However, today I want to address some issues from the NT perspective, in discussing what is being called "Cassandra Phenomenon" or "Ongoing Traumatic Relationship Syndrome." *Disclaimer: I am NOT saying that living with a person on the spectrum will automatically cause OTRS but there are challenges and stressors that come with daily living in a spectrum household. My desire is not to offend or disrespect spectrum persons but to build an understanding of some challenges in the Aspie-NT marriage. This article will reflect more on the NT perspective.*

What is *Cassandra Phenomenon* or OTRS? This term was coined by Families of Adults Affected by Asperger's Syndrome (http://faaas.org/otrscp/), and their website can provide more detail about the history of the name. However, in Greek mythology the basic story of Cassandra was that Apollo gave her the gift of prophecy and foreseeing the future as part of his ploy to seduce her, but when she rejected him by spitting upon him, he cursed her with a curse of never being believed. Cassandra then had the power to accurately predict the future. She would warn and educate about something that was about to happen, but because of the curse she would be dismissed, rejected, or disregarded. The event would come to pass again and again, but the curse of never being believed would be the never-ending source of her pain and frustration in life. (She had forewarned her people about the Trojan horse and was dismissed). The townspeople saw her as insane, mad, and a liar; and eventually, living between this gift and curse ultimately drove her to complete insanity, which was accompanied by incarceration.

Therefore, spouses and parents in a spectrum household identify with this conflict. Let me reflect on a personal experience with my child and the education system.

Although there are countless stories for me to draw upon, the most vivid involves a situation with my daughter's first third-grade teacher. My daughter was diagnosed, she had an IEP (Individualized Education Plan) in place, and I was meeting with the teacher before the start of the school year to discuss her school supplies and where she should be placed for seating (preferential seating as described in the IEP). This teacher had a rule, first of all, that all students would use the same school supplies; the supplies would not be individually owned but shared by the community of students, and all supplies would be the exact color, size, style, and shape, despite any child having a learning need, issue, or challenge. This was issue number one. My daughter is sensory aversive, and using metal handled scissors is a source of discomfort and frustration for her.

I begged and pleaded on her behalf, first of all, for her to be able to keep her supplies in her desk because Aspies do form attachment to their objects and because some of her supplies needed to be different due to her sensory challenges. Specifically, her scissors needed to have a rubber-type padding on them, and her favorite color is blue. This request was denied.

I asked the teacher to show me where she planned for my child to sit. She decided the preferential seat was the seat on the front row, opposite a student, and the desk was close to the exit door. This teacher had desks lined up in rows, facing each other, so the students would be eye-to-eye and have direct contact. There was an odd number of desks, and I found a desk that sat alone on the front row without another desk directly in front it, but deeper into the room away from the exit door. My child had a history of running out of the classroom and a history of breaking her pencils and throwing them out of frustration when the work was overwhelming or the pencil hurt her hand.

I forewarned the teacher that there could be a possible scenario where my daughter would escape class (which later she did, often). Or, if she were using those horrid metal-handled scissors, she might get frustrated, throw them, and risk hitting the student seated in front of her. Out of her sensory issue, not malintent, she would fling the scissors and not take into account that there was another person seated in front of her. The teacher dismissed these concerns and maintained that she was following the IEP, and *she* chose the preferential seat. Within three to four weeks of the start of school, the inevitable happened.

The class was working on a cutting project. Sydney did not want to use the scissors. She was forced to use them, and she got frustrated. The scissors (blunt-edge) went flying by the ear of the student in front of her. The teacher demanded Sydney apologize to the student, pick up the scissors, and resume work. My daughter, who saw situations in black and white, did not see a need to apologize for not hitting the student with the scissors. She didn't want to finish the project, so she remained seated. An assistant was called in, who immediately grabbed my daughter from her seat and attempted to force her to pick up the scissors. Surprised and scared about being picked up from behind, Sydney hit the teacher. When he began to put her in a therapeutic hold, she bit him in her effort to escape.

The call comes to me that I need to pick up my daughter, that she is suspended because she "assaulted a fellow student with scissors, unprovoked, refused to apologize, and hit and bit the assistant for no reason." This event eventually led to her being dismissed from the school and put temporarily into a secluded classroom because she was "too dangerous to be around mainstream students." I attempted to plead my daughter's case and advocate on her behalf. I reminded the teacher that I had forewarned of this exact situation and that this was not entirely Sydney's fault. This entire situation could have been avoided if I had been heard, but instead, the fault was pinned on me. The school psychologist suggested to those present at the meeting, "Perhaps the mother has Munchausen by Proxy." From that point forward, I would try to educate, forewarn, and advise, but if the school psychologist was there I was dismissed as mentally unstable—you know, Munchausen by Proxy.

This was a source of daily, weekly, monthly stress. When I miscarried several times in 2007, the doctors attributed the first to enormous stress levels, and the most stressful thing I dealt with was the school system and constantly being dismissed and not believed. They said Sydney's issue was behavioral and only required discipline, but because the mom (me) was emotionally and mentally imbalanced,

I was causing this behavior, and it was manifesting at school.

This was also happening at church. My daughter was usually delightful at church because she loved it as a child. I would write-up little manuals or guidelines for "what if" scenarios but often would be told, "She may do that at school or home, but she never does that here."

On more than one occasion what I predicted would happen did happen, and the teacher would look at me in disbelief and quickly dismiss the fact that I had predicted the outcome. This is extremely stressful. When you have knowledge and try to forewarn and prevent, then get rejected or dismissed, the stress of wondering when or where something will happen or waiting for that next call is unbearable.

In a marital situation, if the couple is thirty-five years old or older, more than likely the spouse presenting with ASD/Asperger's is undiagnosed. Perhaps a child was diagnosed and then the NT spouse begins to learn about the syndrome/spectrum and sees these same traits in her spouse. She begins to look back on the marriage in hindsight, applying this syndrome to some pretty hurtful times where her husband maybe was inattentive, dismissive, or worse, something happened that could have been prevented had he heeded her warning. She researches this and brings it up to her spouse, but often the Aspie spouse quickly dismisses it. After all, he did marry, is usually pretty successful at his job, and he does not have a disability.

In fact, he says, "Maybe you're the crazy one. You're the one who cries and gets emotionally upset." He says, "I think you are negative and critical, constantly bringing up things I supposedly do that hurt you. We don't need marital counseling. You need counseling."

The pattern continues as the wife begins to read marital books and attend seminars, thinking perhaps she needs to be a better wife. Maybe he's right, that it's all in her head, and she is negative and critical. She's feeling anxious or depressed and seeks counseling. Counseling is not helping. She may decide she needs psychotropic medication to cope with her marriage and life because she feels disconnected with her husband. She feels he does not give empathy. She feels dismissed and that they lack mutual interest or shared enjoyment. Maybe if she tries hard enough things will improve. She may try to discuss her feelings with friends who more than likely have

NT husbands, and they tell her their husbands do similar things (but, trust me, it is nowhere near the level of the Aspie man) that she needs to pray harder, try harder, find ways to work on it. After all, the Aspie spouse usually presents to the public as docile, maybe quiet or naïve, so no one would ever imagine she would feel the pain of isolation and other challenges she is describing.

She may seek spiritual counsel only to be told that if she would be more submissive and respect her husband, she would find contentment and happiness. She has tried everything—counseling, talking, spiritual advice, but something still seems amiss. She may get him to go to marriage counseling because she's not satisfied in marriage and she feels as if maybe she's going crazy. Does she feel what she feels? Does she see what she sees? Is this normal? Does he have this Asperger thing, or is she making it all up?

If the marriage counselor is unfamiliar with ASD, they usually see the Aspie presenting as quite calm and saying, "You know, I'm quite content in this marriage, but she's negative, critical, and so emotional. I think she really needs the help." The wife now has been through years of reading books, attending seminars and counseling, and talking with friends and is presenting as anxious, depressed, and discontent. Nine out of ten times, marriage counseling will be unsuccessful, and things will continue to spiral downward. Studies suggest between 70 and 90 percent of Aspie-NT marriages end in divorce. Hence, what the wife may be experiencing is Cassandra Phenomenon, or OTRS.

To this side of the Aspie-NT equation, it is important first off to validate the concerns and challenges of the NT spouse without a lot of advice giving. After seeing the couple together a time or two, I find it is better to do the majority of the work separately.

The NT spouse needs:

1. Validation: It is very important for the NT spouse to have a safe place to vent and receive care, to communicate and to be heard, and to have her points of frustration understood.
2. Realize that the NT spouse feels trapped, especially if he or she is a Christian. If there is not addiction, physical abuse, or adultery, the NT feels there is no way out, or at the very least he or she is conflicted about wanting to terminate the

relationship.

3. The NT spouse will be conflicted about the diagnosis or possibility of the spouse having Asperger's/ASD. To one point the diagnosis or possibility of a label validates that there are challenges, but since ASD is a permanent challenge, she may feel a sense of hopelessness that anything can be done to bring change in the marriage to a point where the NT feels there will be fulfillment in the marriage. The NT spouse often feels there was a bait and switch. First, they didn't know their partner had ASD. Second, oftentimes when the NT person is the object of the ASD person's affection/obsession, there is much more attention and time spent together during the quest of the relationship during the courtship period. When the focus shifts after marriage, the NT partner is left wondering what happened to the person she dated and fell in love with? Why do they no longer pursue her?

4. The spouse, out of frustration, may want the Aspie spouse "cured" or "fixed." As a parent of an Aspie, I can tell you there is nothing to fix. There is a neurological wiring difference that serves that person well in other areas of life, but which does happen to challenge intimate relationships. Still, the Asperger's/ASD is not *the* root of every problem. Be careful treading here. For mutual marital satisfaction, each spouse will have to learn some compromise. Each spouse will need new communication tools and ways to find satisfaction in the marriage. The NT spouse may be burned out and exhausted, having carried years of hurt and frustration. Be gentle and move slowly, not placing all the responsibility of adaptation on the NT spouse. Aspie/ASD spouses, if motivated, can learn new skills, adapt and modify, but not "change." *Change* is not a word that should be used, as it is very offensive to the person on the spectrum.

5. This is a process. The NT spouse has long been comparing the marriage possibly to a couple of two NTs. The dynamic of Aspie-NT is a different marriage connection, and one has to give up the dream of having an NT-NT marriage with an Aspie spouse. The marriage will be different, but it does not have to be "less than" or unfulfilling.

6. Unfortunately, Aspie spouses can lack motivation to change

and, being that they are not feeling as dissatisfied, may have trouble getting started or making steady progress. This makes the NT spouse feel unimportant and lack security. It is important to help the Aspie spouses understand there are changes and adaptations to be made that he/she will not see as important or valid, but in sacrifice to the one they love if they want their spouse to feel secure, connected, and important, they will need to make some necessary adaptations and modifications.

Cognitive-Behavioral therapy is the main modality to use with the Aspie-NT couple. Modalities that focus on emoting or making the Aspie "feel" certain things will not be effective. Aspies will need to know the logical reasons and explanations of why you are asking them to do or modify certain things. A cognitive, rational approach with some reality therapy will be most effective. This is one side of the marriage equation. In the next article, we will look at the marital equation from the Aspie/ASD point of view.

Complex Cases: Aspie-NT Marriage
What Do Aspies Have to Say About Marriage Counseling?
Stephanie C. Holmes, MA, BCCC
Certified Autism Counselor

In the last article, I wrote about Aspie-NT marriage, and I wrote from the NT side of the equation. This time I turn the tables and see what Aspies (those on the Spectrum) have to say about being married to an NT (neurotypical). Many times it is the NT wife who calls or emails, because she has discovered that perhaps her spouse has Asperger's/ASD. The call is one of desperation, a cry for help. And often the question is, "What can we do to help/fix him?" This article will specifically focus on male Aspies and another will focus on the nuances of having an Aspie wife. I am not Aspie and certainly will not claim to speak on their behalf, so I surveyed Aspies and asked them to share their perspective on Aspie-NT marital relationships.

Literature and research is woefully behind on Asperger's/ASD in adults. As previously stated, older adults who have a child diagnosed or struggling in marriage after several attempts of marital therapy begin to wonder what is so different about them, why isn't their spouse happy, or what is wrong with their spouse? Why are they so critical or negative? The usual marriage therapy modalities do not seem to help this complex case of marital issues.

One of the first things to address is the Cassandra Phenomenon (discussed in the previous Aspie-NT article). If you survey most NT wives, they will assure you that this is real and will be able to identify with the symptoms and feel validated. What do Aspies have to say about this? I surveyed some Aspies for their opinions. The Aspie females were highly offended by the notion of Cassandra Phenomenon and said living with an NT spouse causes Cassandra Phenomenon. What did the Aspie men have to say? This is just a sample:

- I fully accept the claims of NT spouses that suffer with the Cassandra Phenomenon. I see it in my family. I wish it could be otherwise.

- It seems to say that there is not much positive about living with someone with Asperger's. I don't like thinking that living with me would cause that kind of stress. I don't want my spouse to feel that way.
- I feel sorry for them and wish they could understand the helplessness that we feel in the fact that we need to change but can't. Like trying to make yourself two feet taller or to cure yourself of brain cancer.
- I am sure it is very frustrating for NT spouses to feel like they are the problem. It is clearly not fair.
- I am sure this [Cassandra Phenomenon] is highly probable and very true for the NT spouse.
- The phenomenon seems logical and plausible. But whether it is Asperger's or Cassandra's, the question is what to do with it? With Asperger's or Cassandra syndrome, we can live this life while glorifying God because He is the treasure above all treasures (Matthew 13:44).
- It pains me to think my behaviors could cause that kind of an issue, but there are issues living with an NT, as well. They are a different kind altogether.

These responses illustrate that Aspie spouses do feel sympathy and do realize that their Asperger's is causing complex issues in the marriage, but as one said, "The question is what do we do about it?" Asperger's/ASD is a neurological issue. It is a way one is wired, how one simply is. The wonderful thing about the Aspie brain that makes them brilliant in science, technology, engineering, mathematics, and the arts, unfortunately, causes a challenge to relating to others like bosses, spouses, their child, family, employee, and friend.

I asked Aspie spouses if they struggle with any other issue in addition to Asperger's? Common answers:

- Depression
- Social Anxiety
- Collecting (Hoarding)
- ADHD
- Mood Disorder
- OCD

- Generalized Anxiety

What is it like to live with someone who is wired so differently than you, whose expectations for you may compare you to an NT male, or perhaps they base marital expectations on a NT-NT marriage relationship?

- I know that many marriages struggle and many do not make it. I know neurotypicals are heartbroken just as Aspies are. There is no quick fix. This is the hand God calls us to. Only God can heal the heart.
- Aspies don't speak the same language as NTs. When it comes to nonverbal communication, we just don't get it. We have trouble with the verbal part a lot of the time. I spend a lot of time trying to think of the right response to you, so I miss a lot of what you are saying. I want to respond in a way that will please or, at least, not offend. But that's just me. Other Aspies just blurt things out. I have embarrassed myself in the past by saying something inappropriate, so I have learned to compensate.
- She tells me what makes her mad and what upsets her about me but is offended if I share what she does that hurts me. It seems like she thinks that because I have Asperger's, I am the project, that I am the only one who needs to change or "be fixed."
- I struggle with seeing how all marital issues fall on the Aspie. Who is to say the NT way of communicating is the correct way? Why is it wrong or offensive to speak the truth and be direct? Why does she expect me to read her mind or be able to read her body language or tone? Why can't she just tell me what is bothering her or what to do, because I'm certainly not going to guess correctly?
- This relationship can cause me pain, too, and that doesn't seem to count. She misreads my intentions and vilifies my character nearly every argument, but I bring up that her perception is wrong, and I upset her even more. When I try to explain why I did something, I'm just defending myself or being rude. It is important to me for her to understand that

usually the reason she thinks I did or did not do something is usually not accurate. I never intend to hurt her.

- Continued confirmation that I am inadequate in providing emotional and intimate support for my wife and my sons. The fact that I cannot do what it takes to make my wife feel fulfilled and bring her happiness makes me feel like a failure as a husband and father.

- I think the biggest thing is that we really don't understand what NTs mean when they say, "relationship, closeness, and intimacy," because we simply do not have an understanding of what those really feel like. You can define these and, yes, we can understand a description, but since we have never felt any of these, we can't really relate.

All Aspies who participated in the survey said their spouse has remarked more than once that they (NT spouse) either wish they had known about the Asperger's and had never married them, or wish they could separate or divorce from them. The NT spouse often feels they can't divorce due to the conflict of being a Christian and not feeling like this syndrome falls under the biblical reason for a Christian to divorce.

These comments cause pain and wounding and hurt the Aspie spouse. It causes them to feel rejected, like giving up or isolating, or as if it is not possible to ever meet their spouse's expectations. Each Aspie male said they see some positives in Asperger's as far as how the mind thinks about logical or other things, but they feel badly that they are so incompetent in personal relationships. Each one expressed sadness that their spouse feels emotional pain or wounds from their words, behaviors, or lack of initiative for various things. Some Aspie spouses said they felt there was nothing they could really do to help the marriage; others said if they knew what to do they would do it to the best of their ability, but they felt they still would not be able to meet their spouse's expectations.

When I asked these Aspie spouses how soon into the marriage their spouses said something was different or off or they felt discontent, the results varied from one to five years. When I asked the NT spouse at what point they had red flags that something was different or not quite right in the relationship, the response was months to two years.

If you Google or search for info on Aspie-NT marriage, the comments are usually negative, bleak, or do not give much hope. Many blogs are written from the NT point of view after the NT has been in a broken marriage with an Aspie, and the writings stem from hurt, anger, or brokenness. Their advice is to leave or end the marriage—ASAP!

Asperger's entered our vocabulary in 1994. Those persons born since that time are twenty and over and may have never been diagnosed or even suspected they had this syndrome. In surveying wives as to why they were first attracted to their spouse I asked, "What traits attracted you to them?" Responses were:

- "I liked his simplicity, stability, practicability, and his mysterious aloofness as something to pursue. He was tall, dark, and handsome, and faithful to me. We agreed in all the basic areas of life but had to date long-distance until we could get married."
- "Intellectual compatibility, playfulness, respect for my physical boundaries, adventurous spirit to try new restaurants or go exploring, how well he got along with my friends and family ... as if he'd always been a part."
- "He had a boyish kind of innocence. I could see his heart that was so big for people. He was also a cute kind of awkward. We met in college, and his roommate told me he was the most mild guy he'd ever met. His roommate said that when he was mad he would just say, 'I'm mad,' in a calm tone."
- "I admired his stability and the fact that he didn't go out drinking every weekend."
- "I felt comfortable and safe with the humble and gentle demeanor my husband seemed to have, as well as his friendliness and likability with others. He was also very willing to help me and others."
- "He was different, and I liked that he was different and quirky. He was very intelligent, and I felt like he would go far with his chosen career. I knew he loved me and would be faithful to me, and I saw how he interacted with children at church and thought he would make a great dad one day."
- "I was attracted to his quiet and calm nature. He treated me

with respect and seemed secure. It didn't hurt that he had
beautiful dimples and a sincere smile. We had our faith and
music in common, and my children seemed very comfortable
around him."

- "I saw him as kind, dependable, and potentially a faithful
provider. Probably our biggest connecting point is the
enjoyment of outdoor activities. He had a boat, and we both
enjoyed being out on it, picnicking and skiing. We were both
divers. We enjoyed going to outdoor events."

Without even knowing it, the underlying attraction seems to be
to Aspie traits. However, soon into the marriage the NT doesn't feel
connected, or they struggle with intimacy. Usually, it is well into the
marriage, when there are often children, that the wife searches for
what is missing or asks, "Is there a name for this?" Years of
misunderstanding and miscommunication cause deep wounds. From
the counselor point of view, I see that many of the wounds are
caused by expectations, loss of dreams, and misperceiving various
actions or lack of actions from their spouse. Marriage seminars and
books and how-to's in the Christian community are based primarily
on an NT-NT marriage model.

When NT women marry, they set that expectation as the bar and
rarely does the Aspie spouse meet those expectations. There is grief
or anxiety about what the security or stability may look like with an
Aspie spouse. But for years, without a label or name the NT spouse
may have inaccurately assigned a motive or intention behind a
spouse's words or behaviors. Each spouse, whether Aspie or NT,
tends to view reasons from their own point of reference, not from
the other's reference point. This misperception over years and years
underlies the NT spouse's wounds.

Marital therapy where one spouse is Aspie needs to start on a
cognitive-behavioral level. Step one in counseling is often to educate
each spouse about what Asperger's/ASD is and is not. There are
many myths and misperceptions on the Web. It is important for both
spouses to understand that if indeed he has Asperger's, it is a reason
not an excuse for hurtful or even abusive behaviors. Just because he
has Asperger's he does not get a pass. Step two is to explain how the
Aspie brain is wired differently than the NT brain, that when he says
he did not know or pick up something, he probably did not. When

you have to repeat the same thing over and over like you are living in the movie *Groundhog Day*, there is a reason. There is a short-term processing issue.

Step three is to help the Aspie spouse understand how Asperger's impacts the marital relationship, that the NT spouse entered the marriage with certain expectations and she must grieve some of those dreams/expectations so that something new can be achieved. I explain to every couple that what we will work on and create in therapy is not a goal or goals based on NT-NT marriage. We will work on assessing the challenges and strengths of this marriage and examine what the impact of the Asperger's is and is not, and we will move forward from there. I state that the goal of therapy is not to change, fix, or cure the Aspie spouse because that is not achievable. Changing the brain is not the achievable goal. The achievable goal is to build a relationship of adaptations, tweaks, and modifications, wherein both spouses can feel validated and accepted in the marriage.

It is possible, but not the norm, to have abuse in the relationship. This is based on the Aspie's upbringing and whether another issue is co-morbid with the Asperger's, which would complicate matters. If abuse exists, it must be addressed immediately. Marriage therapy in this complex case is a slow process. I do not do every session with the couple together unless they specify it. I usually start with the couple to hear what is happening from each spouse and see how they relate to each other with body language and tone. Then, I try to have the NT spouse come in to share or vent her hurts and wounds and what she would like to say, unfiltered, and free of the fear of hurting feelings or retaliation. I do most of the work one-on-one, with the Aspie spouse asking the NT spouse to email me with incidents or issues that arise during the week. If the NT spouse needs a session to vent or share challenges or share how things are progressing or declining, that is made available. I try to see the spouses together every four to six weeks, optimally, to evaluate progress, ask for measureable goals, and set additional definable goals. Usually we only work on two to three goals at one time. The NT list of goals is usually long, but we start with the basics and we start small and build from there.

Marital happiness and fulfillment is indeed possible if both spouses are able to accept the diagnosis, accept the impact and implications, work together to achieve a marriage where each feels needs are being met, and can let go of the notion of the perfect Christian NT-NT marriage that most marriage books paint a picture of achieving.

The divorce rate is unfortunately high in Aspie-NT marriages. Several of the men I have worked with were in a second or third marriage before being diagnosed or presumed to have Asperger's Syndrome. I asked each person surveyed what they felt was the prognosis for marital happiness in an Aspie-NT marriage, and I liked this answer, "Fortunately, our marriage is based on a commitment rather than a single emotion of 'love.' We are both two broken individuals, each in our own way. We are called to love and accept each other in our own brokenness."

APPENDIX XV

Spectrum Teens: The Issues They Face
An interview with Dr. Tony Attwood
Stephanie C. Holmes, MA, Certified Autism Specialist

Adolescence is a challenging time whether or not you have autism spectrum disorder/Asperger's, but spectrum teens certainly have a few more challenges to face during this already tumultuous stage of life. Currently the rate of ASD diagnosis is ten to one, boys to girls. However, experts in the field such as Dr. Tony Attwood, Dr. Temple Grandin, and Jennifer O'Toole believe that this ratio is wrong. They believe the ratio is probably more than likely closer to four to one, boys to girls. Girls tends to be misdiagnosed or missed altogether because their brain wiring helps them be less conspicuous. However, being less conspicuous in their symptoms does not mean that they struggle less in the adolescent years.

My first question to Dr. Attwood was: What transition points for spectrum teens tend to be the most problematic to them? His answer, pointed and humorous, began with, "First of all, we must remember that those with Asperger's (ASD) do not have an illness or disease from which they suffer. There are not stomachaches or headaches or physical symptoms as such to cause suffering. Those with Asperger's (SD) suffer most because of peer groups around them. Neurotypical teenagers are toxic creatures. Teenagers are toxic to mental health. The suffering endured is not because of Asperger's. It is because of the attitude and degradation of others in the peer group."

Dr. Attwood and I discussed the already changing nature of the academic environment that happens in middle and high school, compared to that of elementary and primary school. These factors add to the stressors of all adolescents but are compounded in the spectrum teen who does not handle change well. In addition to the environment changing to pre-pubescent teenagers, the nature and level of schoolwork is changing. Academic expectations are increased, and more independent work is expected with more complex and abstract concepts to grapple with in middle school. The classwork and homework is expected to be more self-directed and a lecture-only teaching style is not best approach for the mostly visual learning style of the spectrum teen.

To add to this, most teachers begin to assign team or group work and projects, which can set the spectrum teen up for stress, anxiety, and teasing as they work alongside neurotypical teenagers. Another significant change is from the one-teacher classroom in elementary school to a seven-period day with different teachers, different teacher personalities and expectations, and more organization skills required in changing classrooms through the day.

I asked Dr. Attwood to list what he considered to be the highest stressors spectrum teens face outside of changing classwork expectations. His first response was, "An Aspie losing a close friend is a catastrophic event. It is like being in the middle of a tumultuous ocean without a life raft any longer. The friend was the life raft." He added, "A good friend for an Aspie is better than Prozac or any other psychotropic drug. A good friend can change things dramatically for the Aspie. So, the loss of a close friend is one of the worst things that can happen to an Aspie teenager."

The stressors that Dr. Attwood said puts spectrum teens at higher concern for clinical levels of depression and anxiety include, but are not limited to, rejection from peers, humiliation, or bullying and teasing. Dr. Attwood explains that NT teens who get the occasional teasing or rejection from other peer cliques have a social group that helps repair the damage from the cruel words or rejection. If Sally the NT teen is picked on by a group of girls for what she wore or how she did her hair, she has a peer group that comes alongside her and says, "Oh Sally, that's not true. They were just being mean." Or the friends come around her to support her and reaffirm her worth to their group. Aspies or spectrum teens tend to be alone and do not have a group to "offer emotional repair."

"What happens then," explains Dr. Attwood, "is without repair the Aspie teen tends to *believe* what was said and internalize those thoughts. Cruel words are seeds that bear fruit, and they are powerful and wounding. The Aspie believes the bully."

In a conference held in Atlanta, Georgia, in October 2012, Dr. Attwood listed the common causes for clinical levels of depression in Aspie Teens. He said the first factor is being alone or alienated, which can set the Aspie up for being bullied, teased and ridiculed. But another major aspect is trying to act "NT." Dr. Attwood explained, "Most Aspie teens realize they are different. They tend to study their NT peers as if they are studying a play with actors. They try to emulate their NT peers to the best of their ability, and this is emotionally and mentally exhausting." They figure out that the "real me" is different and must not be "good enough," so I need to act or be someone else so that I can "earn" friends. This feeling of being watched and acting can also lead to clinical levels of chronic anxiety where the Aspie teen feels powerless, inferior, and puts constant pressure on themselves to fit in with their peers.

What troubled me most as a mother of an Aspie teen, was when Dr. Attwood stated at the Atlanta conference that one in three Aspie teens have clinical levels of depression and are at risk of "depression attacks" that can come on suddenly and seemingly without warning to NT parents, just as an anxiety attack. I began to take this seriously and research the affects of this clinical depression and found many studies stating suicidal ideation is on the rise among Aspie teens. Dr. Attwood illustrated what could be the perfect storm to trigger a depression attack in the Aspie/spectrum teen. First, we are trying to get Aspie teens to be educated in an environment with teenagers, and that alone is already toxic to overall mental health. Aspies have empathetic attunement, which is an extraordinary "sixth-sense ability" to read negativity in an environment. They may not be able to read faces and pick up on social cues, but they sense when there is danger or negative emotions around them. If the teen is also feeling isolated or being bullied, therein lies the opportunity for a depression attack to be triggered.

Brain research shows that Aspie/spectrum teens have an enlarged amygdala. The amygdala is part of the limbic/emotional system and is part of the fight/flight/freeze reaction system. Their brains also have different wiring in the pre-frontal cortex, which is responsible for understanding actions and long-term consequences and in planning behaviors. Dr. Attwood gave the analogy of a gazelle or other grazing animal on the savannah. If the animal hears a twig snap or senses a predator, the gazelle does not reason out what the options could be as to why it heard the sound. The gazelle goes into survival mode and reacts; it runs from perceived danger. The Aspie/spectrum teen brain has some similar features to this animalistic instinct of survival.

If we take into account an enlarged amygdala—which may overreact to perceived danger or threat—no repair system to help the teen figure out better options, and a pre-frontal cortex that may not be giving messages about permanent consequences to current feelings, the Aspie teen could have a depression attack. Clinicians are trained to recognize warning signs and behaviors of those who may be at risk for suicidal ideation and suicidal tendencies. When you have an Aspie teen who already may have blunted affect, whose routine or grades have not changed, who has not given away prized possessions or thought through a suicide plan in advance, it makes it more difficult to analyze when an Aspie teen is at risk for a depression attack.

Dr. Attwood said, "The Aspie teen could wake up in the morning, and be fine and seem normal to the parents. Then, something happens at school at the beginning of the day that triggers anxiety or negative thoughts and they go into reaction mode. Without a pre-frontal cortex responding that running out of the building into the street in front of the bus could result in a permanent consequence, and the warning system of the brain at hyper-alert, the Aspie teen could be at higher risk to harm themselves or inadvertently kill themselves because of something that happened in that moment."

Aspie/spectrum teens are also at risk for anorexia and gender identity confusion as a result of bullying by same-gender peers, and drug and alcohol consumption in order to self-medicate from feelings of isolation.

I asked Dr. Attwood what he saw as solutions or resources to help Aspie/spectrum teens during this tumultuous time of adolescence. His first suggestion was that Aspie teens have a therapist who is trained in cognitive-behavioral therapy with an understanding of ASD. Even though Asperger's Syndrome is not a disorder that causes depression or anxiety, the treatment by others and the feeling that they are different certainly puts them at a higher risk. Having a trusted person to talk to can be helpful. He said the best medicine and help for Aspie teens is a supportive peer group.

Dr. Attwood travels internationally quite extensively and in his travels he said flight attendants wear pins representing the flag of the language they speak so that international passengers have someone who can interpret and can communicate with those who speak a different language. He feels what would be excellent for Aspies is for school systems to identify safe peers who are able to understand and "speak" Aspie. These safe peers could be taught how to help Aspies navigate the social waters of school life and be a haven to Aspies who might have struggles with social issues during the day.

"Just like these flight attendants wear the pin representing the flag of the language they speak, these safe peers could wear a jigsaw puzzle pin indicating to Aspies that they are safe to communicate with and could be helpful to them." These safe peers could be a buffer between the Aspie and bullies. They could also help the Aspie determine the character of predators and help navigate in dangerous social situations. Best of all, they could help with "repair" work if the Aspie teen has a negative social encounter at school.

It would be amazing and helpful if our school systems would do more to educate students not just "not to bully," but how to reach out to those who are most susceptible to it, how to be a help to them. A popular myth is, "Aspies prefer to be alone." This is not truth. Aspie teens tend to seclude themselves when they are rejected and isolated from the peer group. Creating their own world, obsessions with gaming or reading, is oftentimes an escape or coping skill to feeling alone, and they resign themselves to being alone. They don't choose to be alone.

Dr. Attwood said in a situation where a student is being bullied or teased and it is agonizing to go to school, "Homeschooling them can save lives." As parents and educators, be vigilant of that student that "doesn't quite fit in." Get to them individually and get to know their strengths and what they have to offer to their community. Help them find a way to find a niche at school through clubs or activities. Having a therapist for to work with as a preventative measure is never a bad idea, and helping to create positive peer relationships can help them tremendously.

Reprinted with permission from Autism/Asperger's Digest.

APPENDIX XVI

Christian Counseling Article
Treatment-Resistant Issues: Perhaps a Red Flag for Autism Spectrum Disorder (Asperger's Syndrome)
An interview with renowned Asperger's expert: Dr. Tony Attwood
Stephanie C. Holmes, MA, BCCC,
Certified Autism Specialist

The long awaited updates to the DSM were released with great anticipation in May 2013. Even for clinicians, change is never easy. The changes in the DSM-5 are greatly applauded by some and criticized by others. Perhaps the loudest outcry came from the Autism/Asperger's community, and I was one of those voices. Various studies conducted through Autism Speaks and other organizations point out there is good reason for the concern as it pertains to the diagnostic criteria of the new category broadly called autism spectrum disorder in the DSM-5.

There are two major things that have upset clinicians and educators who work with persons on the spectrum:

1. The removal of PDDNOS and Asperger's Syndrome. Scientific studies reviewing and researching the new diagnostic terms show that it is these two groups of individuals that appear to be excluded from the new criteria. This is primarily problematic in services to be received in the school setting. For those previously diagnosed with PDDNOS or Asperger's who were receiving services, most are being "grandfathered in" to the ASD diagnosis and still receiving services. The issue becomes the thousands who could have received services but now may be excluded with the new diagnostic criteria.

2. The change from three major criteria in DSM-IV-TR to two criteria in the DSM-5. In the previous manual, there were three criteria in which to judge if a person showed autistic characteristics: social skills, communication, and repetitive or restricted behaviors. In the new manual there are now only

two, as social skills and communication have been combined into one criterion. That may seem subtle, but that is a big change. Also, in the DSM-5 there is a stricter criterion for what meets the standard of a repetitive or restrictive behavior. This is also problematic because how one demonstrates their restrictive behavior may be dependent on his/her temperament, home environment, access to therapies, or current support in managing those behaviors.

The clinical community, which is tasked with revising the DSM, is also given the responsibility of classifying and researching what symptoms make up a disorder or diagnosis, which in turn gives clinicians a common language for classifying and treating clients and patients. What this manual determines as the guidelines for diagnosis then impacts how insurance is billed and what services a person can receive in a school or job setting. As clinicians, it is certainly important to make a diagnosis based on the current criteria. I want to mention some red flags or other issues that may point you in a direction of ASD not mentioned in the DSM-5 or its predecessors.

I recently had a wonderful opportunity to interview world-renowned Asperger's syndrome expert, Dr. Tony Attwood, who resides and practices in Brisbane, Australia, for an article in *Autism Digest*. Dr. Attwood and I discussed issues of growing concern in the spectrum teen community and concern that clinicians may not be aware of when working with this population.

Founding editor of the *European Child and Adolescent Psychiatry*, Professor Lars Christopher Gillberg, said eating disorders, specifically anorexia nervosa, are a huge concern in Aspie/spectrum females. Gillberg's research suggests that in many cases, counting calories, obsession with exercise, or foods the client will or will not eat are often part of the "restricted or repetitive pattern" criteria for ASD.

Dr. Attwood responded: "Traditionally, family and group therapies are the treatments of choice in typical anorexia, but for a person with Asperger's Syndrome struggling with what appears to be anorexia, these treatments simply will not work." Gillberg's research suggests that if a client who has been diagnosed as anorexic appears to be resisting traditional treatment, it is plausible to consider the client may have undiagnosed Asperger's Syndrome. Therefore, one-to-one cognitive-behavioral therapy is more effective to break the rules and obsessions with food or calorie counting.

It is important to note the current rate of ASD diagnosis of males to females is ten to one. Leading experts such as Attwood, Gillberg, Baker and others, believe Aspie girls are being missed and the ratio is closer to four to one. In August 2013, research by Autism Research Center at the University of Cambridge used MRIs to compare male and female ASD brains. Some notable results of the study include:

- "As expected the tests found that the brain anatomies of females with autism were substantially different when compared to the brains of their male counterparts. In fact, a completely different set of regions were implicated in the male autism brain than in female autism brains."
- "In terms of brain morphology, females with autism look more alike to typical developing males when compared to typical developing females."
- "So the brain change in females [with ASD] is actually shifting toward typical developing males."

However, just because a female may be less conspicuous in her symptomology does not mean that she struggles less in adolescence than her male counterparts. Research is showing a rise of anorexia among ASD females. With ASD there are already some sensitivities around food: to its smell, texture, and color. Dr. Attwood points out that an Aspie female may have a "special or restricted interest" in food and/or calories, and it could appear to be "typical anorexia," but if the anorexia seems to be treatment resistant, there is cause to think that female may have Asperger's with a "restricted interest" focused on food.

In an effort to fit in, the spectrum female may arrive at an irrational thought, *If only I were thinner, I would be more popular with my peer group.*

Dr. Attwood said, "Remember, Aspies *never* do things in halves." So what can begin with efforts to be thinner can quickly turn to a restrictive interest in food and calorie count. To Dr. Attwood and researchers, this is a manifestation of anxiety in the form of food as a special interest. Dr. Attwood said, "Usual treatment for anorexia is group therapy or a group home or family sessions, but if the female is

Aspie, this style of therapy will not work, and it would be easy to assume the anorexia is treatment-resistant."

Spectrum females are not going to get the same help from groups because their motivation, their focus for the starvation, is different than their neurotypical peers. Dr. Attwood said if the female is on the spectrum, an individual approach to therapy with a logical cognitive-behavioral approach is the best approach for those individuals that seem not to be responding to traditional treatment.

Another area of concern that can be quite the political hot topic is gender identity issues among spectrum teens. You may be aware there are states that have laws concerning counselors addressing gender issues with a person under the age of eighteen. Dr. Attwood stated that research is showing there is a high probability of gender confusion issues with spectrum teens, but it is qualitatively different than what we tend to think of as "gender issues." Because persons on the spectrum tend to be isolated and rejected by their peers, spectrum teens are at higher risk for clinical anxiety, depression, and self-esteem issues. Females on the spectrum tend to be bullied or humiliated by NT female peers. As discussed before, they may reason that becoming thinner and developing a restrictive interest in food is a way to fit in, but if the female does not seem to be able to fit in she may think, *If I were a boy, I would not be bullied so much if I could just be a boy.* Remember, the ASD female brain tends to be wired more like a neurotypical male, and she finds it easier to fit it and socialize with males, instead of understanding the fickle nature of NT females.

Spectrum males are also bullied, teased, and harassed, mostly by NT males. Spectrum males tend to find it easier to find acceptance with NT females. These spectrum males may develop a restricted interest in all things female, believing, *If I became a girl I would be more popular and have better social skills.*

Dr. Attwood encourages clinicians, "Be aware that there are different pathways to the same profile. See if the Aspie teen may believe that if they change their gender or identity it would solve all of their social problems." So, it is of great concern that spectrum teens tend to be naïve and to not understand who can be trusted; and if a peer group such as a gay/lesbian/transgender group were more accepting of them, it would be easier for them to believe that they, too, have gender confusion. The motivation and treatment is again logical, cognitive-style therapy to help the spectrum teen identify irrational thoughts about changing gender to solve all social problems.

Spectrum persons tend to realize they are different and become aware of their social difficulties in adolescence. Adolescence is a challenging time, whether or not you have autism spectrum disorder/Asperger's, but spectrum teens certainly have a few more challenges to face during this tumultuous stage of life. Dr. Attwood stated, "First of all, we must remember that those with Asperger's (ASD) do not have an illness or disease from which they suffer. There are not stomachaches or headaches or physical symptoms, as such, to cause suffering. Those with Asperger's suffer most because of peer groups around them. Neurotypical teenagers are toxic creatures. Teenagers are toxic to mental health. The suffering endured is not because of Asperger's, it is because of the attitude and degradation of others in the peer group."

Dr. Attwood and I discussed the already changing nature of the academic environment that happens in middle and high school from primary and elementary school. These factors add to the stressors of all adolescents but are compounded in the spectrum teen.

In addition to the environment changing to pre-pubescent teenagers, the nature and level of schoolwork is changing. Academic expectations are increased and more independent work is expected with more complex and abstract concepts to grapple with in middle school. The classwork and homework is expected to be more self-directed and a lecture-only teacher style is not best approach for the mostly visual learning style of the spectrum teen. To add to this, most teachers begin to assign team or group work and projects, which can set the spectrum teen up for stress, anxiety, and teasing as they work alongside the neurotypical teenagers. Another significant change is from the one-teacher classroom in elementary education to a seven-period day with different teachers, different teacher personalities and expectations, and more organization skills required in changing classrooms through the day.

Spectrum teens find solace and relief from anxiety in their restricted or special interest. Females tend to be more aware of their social difficulties and confusion, and they may act out with anorexic behaviors, have gender identity issues, or suffer in silence. Females may be more prone to self-harm and self-mutilation. Males tend to be more intense in motion and may act out more destructively. Both male and female spectrum teens could opt to deal with their differences by developing low self-esteem or arrogance and superiority as coping mechanisms, none of which help their social status.

Males on the spectrum may develop special interests in weapons, the military, first-person shooter games, or role-play fantasy games. Dr. Attwood explained, "It is important to understand that the studies that reveal that first-person shooter/violent video games have no adverse affects on teenagers were done on NT teenagers. We need these studies to address Aspie and ASD teenagers, but there is a different effect. If you are being bullied and feel powerless you may develop that interest in something that gives power and protection, like guns. Watching violent movies or movies with retribution can be seen as a documentary on how to behave."

Dr. Attwood also warned about exposure to pornography for spectrum males. He said it is worse than what we typically refer to as *addiction* when the Aspie male's special interest becomes pornography because, again, they can see that as a script on how to treat women with whom they become romantically involved.

Jennifer O'Toole, speaker and author, has warned that Aspie females are more likely to be involved in a relationship of domestic violence. If the Aspie female wants to fit in and is desperate to find a boyfriend for some means of acceptance, her naïveté and lack of perception of danger will leaver her susceptible to finding Mr. Wrong and getting involved in a dangerous dating situation.

Jennifer tells therapists, "If you have a female client who has struggled with or struggles with anorexia, and has a history of violent or abusive dating relationships, and has clinical anxiety or depression, you may want to consider that she has Asperger's syndrome."

As American therapists, we certainly need to abide by criteria of the DSM-5 for diagnosis, but experts around the world who still use the terminology *Asperger's* are providing excellent research materials to help identify these individuals, so that we can give them the best care and treatment. As Christian therapists, we need to educate our community and churches about accepting people with differences such as Asperger's/ASD so that the church and Christian community can be a healing balm to those who not only suffer with ASD but suffer from rejection and isolation in the world.

Reprinted with permission from the American Association of Christian Counselors' blog.

Coming This Fall!

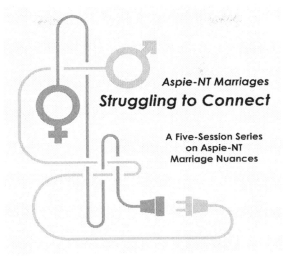

Aspie-NT Marriages
Struggling to Connect

A Five-Session Series
on Aspie-NT
Marriage Nuances

This series seeks to bring light to this marriage dynamic without overgeneralizing or marginalizing the complexities experienced in the Aspie-NT marriage, as well as represent both halves of the marital equation as equally and respectfully as possible.

Series in production to be released fall of 2015:

•**Spectrum Teens and the Issues They Face**

•**Impact of ASD on the Marriage and Family: Moving Beyond Survivng to Thriving**

For information on how to order this series,
as well as additional series,
visit **CounselorStephanieHolmes.com**.